GW00692133

DEVON

COUNTY

COUNCIL

ENGINEERING

AND

PLANNING

DEPARTMENT

TRAFFIC CALMING GUIDELINES

ACKNOWLEDGEMENTS

This book has been compiled by the Engineering and Planning Department of Devon County Council in conjunction with Tim Pharoah.

Edward Chorlton,
County Engineer and Planning Officer
Michael Hatt,
Head of Environment and Planning Services

Project Team
Malcolm Baker, Tim Pharoah, Gerald Shapley, Dick Taylor

Graphic Design and Illustrations
Geraldine Mead, Graham Moores, Mike Harding, Chris Wakefield

Substantial contributions have been made by:
Sam Atrakchi, Mike Bailey, Richard Chaffe, Geoff Downes, Doug Fremlin, Graham Heath, Tim Hipwell, Seumas Lavery, John Manson, Don Millgate, David Netherway, Martin Pay, Edward Paynter, Bernie Richardson, Neil Rugg, Alan Stone, Tony Symes

Special thanks are due to:
Deborah Martin (Proof reading and editorial advice)
Sandra Clarke, Sandra Courtney, Pauline Hilliard, Judith King, Vivien Masterson, Melody Scott, Melanie Tancock (Typing and word processing)
Therese Seward (Office services)
London Borough of Haringey, Leicester City Council, Sheffield City Council, London Borough of Wandsworth and Derek Turner, Hertfordshire County Council (For their help in the preparation of case studies in Section Four)

Thanks are also extended to everyone who has been consulted for information or advice during the compilation of this book or has helped in other ways.

First published in Great Britain in 1991 by:
Devon County Council,
Engineering and Planning Department
Copyright © Devon County Council, 1991
ISBN : 1 - 85522 - 077 - 6

All rights reserved. No part of this publication may be reproduced, stored in a retrieval system, or transmitted in any form or by any means, electronic, mechanical, photocopying, recording or otherwise, without the prior permission of the copyright holder.

Printed and bound in Great Britain by
Smart Print, Exeter
Printed on environmentally friendly paper

FOREWORD

Traffic calming is going to play a major role in our planning for the future.

Motor transport has revolutionised our lives but has brought with it many disadvantages. Traffic calming seeks to put some of these right, particularly in shopping and residential areas. Vulnerable road users such as pedestrians and cyclists, including children, need to be protected and our environment defended.

I am delighted to be part of Devon County Council's initiative and my Committee are sure that this will lead to a better deal for all of us. The information provided will be useful not only for professionals but to the community at large, without whose involvement the initiative cannot succeed.

Councillor Peter Halse
Chairman
Planning and Transportation Committee
Devon County Council

Devon was one of the pioneering counties in the field of traffic calming, gaining early experience in the mid 1980s with a scheme at Burnthouse Lane in Exeter. Since then techniques have been developed and experience has grown.

As with all new techniques it is important to share experience and learn from results. This book has been designed to help people, both within and outside Devon, benefit from both Devon and European traffic calming techniques.

The book illustrates ways in which traffic calming can be achieved and is designed to stimulate thought leading to action rather than to set out a series of rules. All situations vary and it is the design that both improves safety and enhances the appearance of the environment, whilst allowing essential use by vehicles, that will ultimately determine the success of the scheme.

Ideas are presented to help all those involved in the design process to work together to produce schemes that will truly enhance and perhaps in many cases restore the quality of Devon's urban environment.

I wish to thank most warmly Mr Tim Pharoah MSc, MRTPI, MCIT, MIHT of the South Bank Polytechnic for his valuable assistance. He made a major contribution to the preparation of the guidelines as well as providing many of the photographs. His extensive knowledge of the subject, especially of projects throughout Europe, has enabled the results of experience from several countries to be included.

Edward Chorlton.

Edward Chorlton
County Engineer and Planning Officer
Devon County Council

CONTENTS

INTRODUCTION

1.1 The County Council has introduced traffic calming measures at various locations throughout the County. Pedestrian priority in shopping areas, environmental improvements and road safety schemes which incorporate speed reducing techniques have all proved effective in controlling traffic and improving road safety and the living environment. There is now a need to expand on these initiatives, taking account of experience gained in Devon, the rest of the country and abroad. These guidelines set out the present position and give advice on the implementation of future schemes.

THE NEED FOR TRAFFIC CALMING

1.2 The quality of life in our towns and villages is under growing pressure from the increasing volume and use of motor vehicles. As more space is turned over to parked or moving vehicles, less space is available for other activities, while those activities that remain are subject to

1

1: Pedestrianised area of Plymouth creating a pleasant environment for shoppers and office workers. (Photo: Devon County Council)

"Many urban roads and other public areas can offer space for people to meet, rest and enjoy the open air...."

2: Exeter High Street before pedestrian priority scheme. (Photo: Devon County Council)

3: Exeter High Street after pedestrian priority scheme. (Photo: Devon County Council)

4: Inconvenience for pedestrians, the so-called "severence effect" of main roads. (Photo: T. Pharoah)

2

3

4

increasing dangers, noise and fumes. Many streets are now carrying volumes of traffic for which they were never intended and to which they are entirely unsuited. The high performance of modern vehicles can result in speeds and driving behaviour which is potentially dangerous and intimidating for vulnerable road users. Pedestrians, especially children, the elderly and those with a handicap, together with cyclists, are most affected and have almost literally been forced off the road. Many urban roads and other public areas can offer space for people to meet, rest and enjoy the open air and should not be places from which people retreat because of traffic.

1.3 The growing use of the car has also set in motion a vicious circle in which alternative means of travel become less used, less attractive and less viable, which in turn results in further dependence on the car. It is apparent that the full potential growth in car use cannot be accommodated even if such a course was desirable. Ways need to be found to limit the growth of traffic.

1.4 There is a need to change priorities in the way our streets and public spaces are designed and managed so that they can play a useful role and make life more enjoyable in towns and villages. Transport and traffic policy in built-up areas has to be aimed at improving safety and environmental quality rather than the accommodation of more and faster traffic.

However, the routes that carry the majority of traffic, including through trips, do require specific attention to enable them to perform their intended function. In Devon to assist in this process a strategy has been developed to deal with traffic congestion,

5

6

" ways need to be found to civilise or calm traffic especially in residential and shopping areas....."

5: Segregating traffic can at best be only a limited answer; at worst a pedestrian's nightmare. (Photo: T. Pharoah)

6: Service vehicles are an essential part of the commercial scene, and can mix with other street activities. Groningen, Netherlands. (Photo: T. Pharoah)

including the identification of peak pressure routes.

LIMITATIONS OF TRADITIONAL APPROACHES

1.5 The traditional approach to the problem of traffic in towns has generally been to cater for growing traffic while attempting to minimise the environmental damage. This is unsustainable in the long term while leaving major problems unsolved in the short term.

1.6 Attempts to segregate traffic from sensitive areas have been successful in particular cases (e.g. pedestrian shopping streets and village by-passes), but frequently residential and shopping streets have been pressed into service as traffic routes entirely out of keeping with their function and character. Segregation of traffic is often not possible, and cannot provide a universal answer. Traffic ultimately seeks access to the streets in which we live, work and shop, so ways need to be found to civilise or calm

traffic especially in residential and shopping areas.

1.7 One-way streets, road closures and other traffic management measures can create inconvenient access to property. Traffic calming aims to maintain direct access whilst deterring "rat runs".

1.8 The design and appearance of streets has historically been influenced by the requirements of traffic engineering

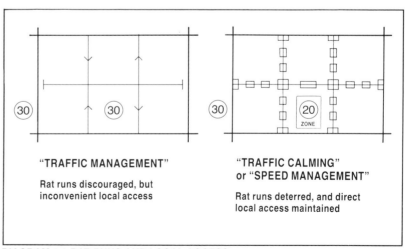

"TRAFFIC MANAGEMENT"
Rat runs discouraged, but inconvenient local access

"TRAFFIC CALMING"
or "SPEED MANAGEMENT"
Rat runs deterred, and direct local access maintained

DIAGRAM 1.1 RAT RUNS AND LOCAL ACCESS

"there is a clear and unequivocal link between speed and the severity of accidents...."

7: Townscape dominated by traffic layout, signs and markings. London. (Photo: T. Pharoah)

8: Surplus carriageway space is unsightly, and can encourage speeding and double parking. (Photo: T. Pharoah)

7

8

geometry, traffic signs, and other street furniture. Some street space consists of carriageway which is surplus to what is useful to traffic, but which is sterile in terms of other possible uses.

1.9 The control of the speed of vehicles has been a problem in many situations. Blanket provisions of 30 mph or 40 mph speed limits are often not respected by a considerable number of drivers and effective enforcement places too great a demand on Police resources. Streets which have been laid out with generous dimensions allow rather than inhibit excessive speed. From a road safety viewpoint, there is a clear and unequivocal link between speed and the severity of accidents. In most urban streets speeds of 30 mph or more are inconsistent with road safety objectives whereas speeds lower than 30 mph generally result in less severe accidents. The chance of a pedestrian sustaining fatal injuries following a collision

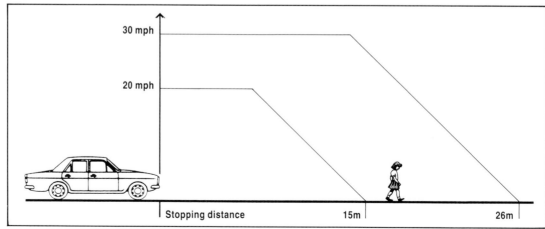

DIAGRAM 1.2 SLOWER IS SAFER

is significantly reduced when vehicle speeds are below 20 mph. Comparative stopping distances for 20 mph and 30 mph are illustrated in Diagram 1.2 .

OBJECTIVES OF TRAFFIC CALMING

1.10 The term "traffic calming" is open to interpretation, but it conveys the basic objective, which is to reduce the adverse effects of road traffic. The approach is to adapt the volume, speed and behaviour of traffic to the primary functions of the streets through which it passes, rather than to adapt streets to the unbridled demands of motor vehicles. The immediate environment needs to convey to the motorist that it would be wholly inappropriate and anti-social to drive at other than a low speed.

1.11 Traffic calming techniques such as those described in these guidelines can directly improve the safety and environmental quality of streets in built-up areas and, in combination with other policies, can help to limit the growth of traffic and promote the use of alternative means of travel with the associated environmental benefits.

1.12 The main beneficiaries of traffic calming are those who live, shop and make their living in frontage properties, and also the most vulnerable people who use the area. The principal aim is to achieve driving speeds and behaviour that are in sympathy with non-traffic activities. This can be done by creating a more constant traffic speed at an appropriate lower level, minimising

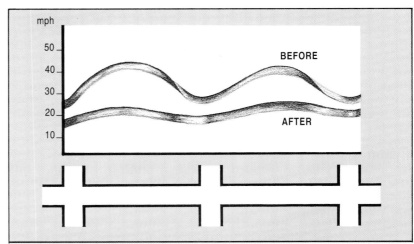

DIAGRAM 1.3 SPEED PROFILE BEFORE AND AFTER CALMING

9

"The principal aim is to achieve driving speeds and behaviour that are in sympathy with non-traffic activities...."

9: In Bedford Street Exeter, traffic is restricted to vehicles requiring access. (Photo: Devon County Council)

braking and acceleration and thus reducing noise and pollution. The aim is also to discourage unnecessary vehicle intrusion into sensitive areas by using techniques that support and enhance the essential character of the area, and which avoid the clutter usually associated with traffic management techniques. Slower speeds also enable some traffic space to be returned to non-traffic uses which can promote local economic and cultural life such as street cafes, street theatre and other open air activities. Traffic calming thus fits well with the concept of street enhancement, encouraging a sense of pride in the urban environment and discouraging litter and graffiti.

1.13 The objectives of traffic calming may be summarised as follows:-

• Improve safety and convenience for vulnerable road users, including pedestrians, cyclists and handicapped people
• Reduce number and severity of accidents
• Reduce noise and air pollution
• Provide space for non-traffic activities (e.g. rest and play)
• Enhance street appearance and reduce the number of traffic signs
• Provide more planting and greenery
• Promote local economic and cultural activity
• Implement improvements in public transport
• Achieve an overall improvement in the environment
• Discourage non-essential use of unsuitable routes by motor vehicles

SPEED/PRIORITY CLASSIFICATION OF ROADS

LIVING AREAS

Walking, cycling and other "living" functions have priority over motor vehicles.
Speed limits to be self-enforcing by the introduction of physical measures.

SUB 20 MPH AREAS
• Pedestrian areas (vehicles mostly excluded)
• Shared-surface streets with little traffic

20 MPH LIMIT AREAS
• Residential and other streets with no through traffic
• "Collector" streets connecting to the traffic areas, but not designated as through routes

MIXED PRIORITY AREAS

Areas where priority is shared between "living" and "traffic" functions including sections of through routes.

20 MPH OR 30 MPH LIMIT (PREFERABLY SELF-ENFORCING)
• Shopping areas, areas near schools, colleges, and other major generators of pedestrian traffic. The use of an area by vulnerable road users, e.g. school children, should weigh heavily in favour of a 20 mph speed limit (with necessary physical measures)

TRAFFIC AREAS

30 MPH LIMIT (NOT NECESSARILY SELF-ENFORCING)
• Signposted major access and through routes such as peak pressure routes where traffic function takes priority, but where vulnerable road users are to be protected
NB. Roads with speed limits higher than 30 mph not included.

TABLE 1

POLICY FRAMEWORK

1.14 The objectives of traffic calming can be realised through three principal measures, namely:-
- Reducing traffic speed
- Reallocating carriageway space to non-traffic activities
- Redesigning and enhancing the street environment

These measures usually involve permanent street works that may have effects beyond the particular street being treated, such as the displacement of traffic from one street to another. Wider transport and town planning considerations are inevitably involved and therefore it is essential that traffic calming is set within a coherent policy framework which needs to have regard to the financial and staff resource implications. The guidelines for "Urban Safety Management" produced by the Institution of Highways and Transportation is a valuable reference in the determination of the policy framework, giving advice on a structured approach to accident prevention and casualty reduction on urban roads.

1.15 A suitable framework can be provided by the re-classification of the roads in built-up areas. This classification should be based on "speed management" and the functions and sensitivity of the roads rather than on traffic function alone. 20 mph speed limit zones are relevant in appropriate situations. The recommended classification framework is shown in Table 1.

10

" it is essential that traffic calming is set within a coherent policy framework...."

10: In Exeter's High Street traffic is confined to mini-buses. (Photo: Devon County Council)

1.16 Unlike traditional road hierarchies, there is no need for the network of roads of any particular speed or set of priorities to be continuous, as illustrated in Diagram 1.4. Changes of speed limits, however, should be kept to a minimum to avoid a proliferation of signs.

1.17 The classification should be drawn up on the basis of existing and planned intentions for each road in the built-up areas. These need to take account of a range of transport and land use policy issues. Once established, the classification itself provides a framework within which these policies, including traffic calming, can be developed. The classification assists in the setting of design, maintenance and other standards, the allocation of resources, and the choice of appropriate traffic calming measures for each road. Decisions need to be taken on the design of new roads and new estates from the outset.

SPECIFIC POLICY ISSUES

1.18 Traffic calming is essentially a better way of resolving different and sometimes competing interests within the street, such as those illustrated in Diagram 1.5. This calls for an integrated approach within which individual policies can be developed. Specific policy issues which can be developed and reviewed in the light of traffic calming objectives and the speed management framework are briefly discussed below.

(a) Road Safety

1.19 The Government's Urban Road Safety Project identified the need for a strategy for the planning and implementation of road safety measures.

This strategy involves the definition of a road hierarchy enabling a degree of redistribution of traffic and safety improvements on selected roads which will result in improved conditions for vulnerable road users. The approach in Devon emphasizes that speed reduction and priority for vulnerable road users needs to be taken into account when determining road safety schemes. As an example, in the "living" areas, self enforcing 20 mph speed limits with supporting environmental improvements are an appropriate road safety technique. In "mixed priority" and "traffic" areas there needs to be a combination of innovative traffic calming measures and more conventional accident prevention treatments.

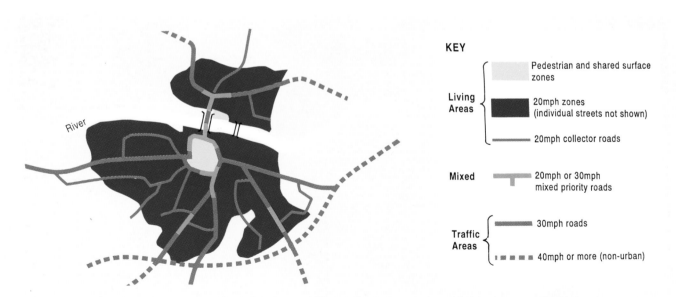

DIAGRAM 1.4 EXAMPLE OF ROAD CLASSIFICATION BASED ON "SPEED MANAGEMENT" FUNCTIONS AND SENSITIVITY

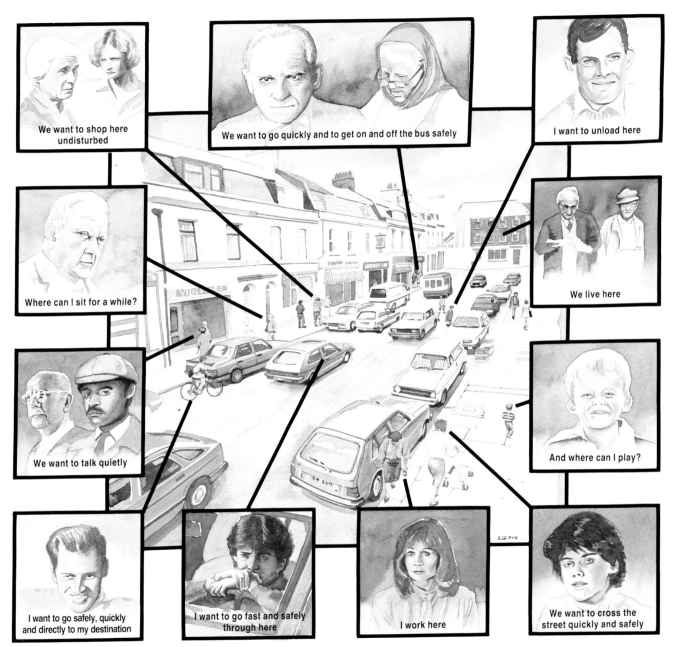

We want to shop here undisturbed

We want to go quickly and to get on and off the bus safely

I want to unload here

Where can I sit for a while?

We live here

We want to talk quietly

And where can I play?

I want to go safely, quickly and directly to my destination

I want to go fast and safely through here

I work here

We want to cross the street quickly and safely

DIAGRAM 1.5 COMPETING ACTIVITIES IN THE STREET

11: Burnthouse Lane, Exeter incorporates flat top humps, sheltered parking and well-defined cycle lanes. (Photo: Devon County Council)

12: The Exe Cycle Route segregates cyclists from other vehicles to their mutual benefit. The route runs parallel to the Exeter canal for some of its length. (Photo: Devon County Council)

13: Lorries using unsuitable routes not only cause congestion but have a detrimental effect on the environment. (Photo: Devon County Council)

11

13

12

(b) Public Transport

1.20 The design of traffic calming measures needs to have regard for any requirements to give priority to public transport. The development of park and ride is also important, and relates well to traffic calming objectives.

(c) Traffic Restraint

1.21 Our streets can no longer be expected to accommodate all the potential traffic growth. Traffic calming strategies can help to limit growth in the "living" areas by discouraging the use of unsuitable roads by through traffic, can allocate priority between different road users in the "traffic" areas, and can contribute to other traffic restraint policies such as parking policy and provision for buses, cycles and pedestrians.

(d) Pedestrians and Cyclists

1.22 The road classification should take account of where pedestrians and cyclists need protection, and where they should be given priority over motor traffic. The further aim is to identify ways of encouraging these modes of travel as alternatives to the car, including the provision of special routes and other facilities. It may be desirable to prepare separate plans for the development of pedestrian and cycle route networks.

(e) Safe Routes to School

1.23 The reduction in child pedestrian casualties is a specific target of traffic calming. The road classification needs to take account of school routes, and local traffic calming schemes should pay special attention to the safety of these routes.

14

15

14: The use of block paving and raised planters help to minimise the visual effect of these parked vehicles in Shilhay, Exeter. (Photo: Devon County Council)

15: Extended pavements, tree planting and seating create an attractive setting at The Plains, Totnes. (Photo: Devon County Council)

(f) Lorry Control and Routeing

1.24 Lorries pose a particular difficulty in view of their environmental impact. The practical advice contained in "Lorries and Traffic Management" published in 1990 by the Civic Trust, County Surveyors' Society and the Department of Transport needs to be used to determine methods of reducing the impact of lorries while maintaining local accessibility.

(g) Parking

1.25 Traffic calming schemes should include provision for on-street and other parking, but should not be devised solely to increase parking capacity. Planting and other features in traffic calming schemes should be used to reduce the visual intrusiveness of parked vehicles. Where parking demand is heavy, imaginative design is required together with appropriate regulations.

(h) Environmental Enhancement

1.26 Traffic calming involves changing the way in which streets are used, and this means that people's perceptions of the street environment also need to change. The appearance and design of streets therefore need to be enhanced to convey to drivers that slow speeds and tolerant behaviour are necessary, and to create a comfortable and attractive environment so that pedestrians, cyclists, residents and others are able to enjoy the new freedoms that traffic calming offers. Environmental enhancement is also necessary to secure public acceptance of the speed reduction measures and other changes. Within the "living" areas, slow speeds mean that generally the need for traffic signs and lane markings is reduced. In these areas design is influenced by the character of the surroundings, rather than by traffic requirements. In the "traffic" areas with speed limits of 30 mph or more, traffic regulations and standards continue to be necessary.

(i) Economic Development

1.27 Areas free from the dangers and disruption caused by traffic have greater potential for economic growth and development. Pedestrianisation and the calming of essential access routes can therefore be used as positive encouragement to shopping and other commercial activity.

(j) Planning Policy

1.28 Land use policy and development control and other planning activity such as housing improvement programmes can make a positive contribution to traffic calming objectives. As an example, land use which generates high traffic volumes should be located in relation to "traffic priority" roads. Traffic calming has an important part to play where buildings and activities are planned around the street frontage and the street block as positive urban features. Although traffic calming measures will be used primarily in existing streets, similar techniques may be applicable to new highway layouts which serve residential and retail developments. However with new developments the aim is to integrate all elements of the design. To obtain futher information on standards for new adoptable residential streets, together with general advice on layouts, it will be necessary to refer to the Devon County Council published "Residential Estates Design Guide". Further review of planning policies and practice with the District Councils may be appropriate to enable the full potential of traffic calming to be realised.

COUNTY COUNCIL TRAFFIC CALMING POLICY

1.29 The County Council has adopted the following traffic calming policies:

(a) Reduce the dominance of traffic in inappropriate streets through physical restraints and environmental enhancement measures

(b) Ensure that the needs of vulnerable road users receive priority and reorganise the street scene to accomplish this objective

(c) Incorporate traffic calming as an accident prevention measure wherever appropriate

(d) Develop public transport and park and ride schemes to cater for predicted traffic demands, and use SCOOT or electronic control systems to extract maximum capacity from the strategic urban network

(e) Ensure that essential lorry traffic is managed with minimum disbenefits to the environment

(f) All new developments should incorporate traffic calming measures where appropriate.

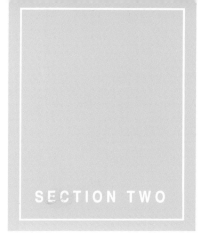

PUBLIC INVOLVEMENT

Purpose

2.1 The key to successful traffic calming is acceptance by the local community. The best way in which this can be achieved is for local interests to be involved in the preparation, design and implementation of schemes. Such involvement serves several purposes:-

- The local community needs to feel that it has played a part in achieving the benefits that the scheme will bring
- The different and sometimes conflicting interests in the area need to be fully considered during the design process of each scheme
- The designers themselves need to have the benefit of local knowledge and ideas
- A wider understanding and acceptance of the purpose and benefits of the scheme can be promoted
- Public responses can assist in the preparation of annual traffic calming programmes

Those Who Need to Be Involved

2.2 The range of bodies involved depends on the scale and type of scheme being planned, but should be as wide as possible.

2.3 Formal consultations are required with the Police, Fire and Ambulance Services. They will make their own requirements known and be able to give helpful advice. Other bodies to be consulted include Statutory Undertakers and Bus Operators.

1: Publicity leaflets used during the Enhancement Programme for Sidmouth Town Centre. (Photo: Devon County Council)

2.4 The District, Town and Parish Councils have an important role in the public participation process. Informal officer consultation is an important step in agreeing schemes with District Councils. The local County and District Councillors for the area should always be kept informed, and they should be invited to any public meetings which may be arranged. It is also helpful for a scheme to have the backing of a well-known and respected local figure. There may be opportunities for joint schemes to be undertaken with the District Councils, particularly when the traffic calming scheme involves a substantial element of environmental enhancement.

Where traffic calming measures are to be implemented as part of a new development, consultations are carried out through the planning process conducted by the District Councils.

2.5 It is also important to establish a dialogue with those who live or work in or otherwise use the area. Residents' groups, civic societies, chambers of trade and commerce and other representatives of particular interests can play a valuable part. Where appropriate local traders and schools should be included in the consultation process.

2.6 Improving road safety is one of the main objectives of traffic calming and the

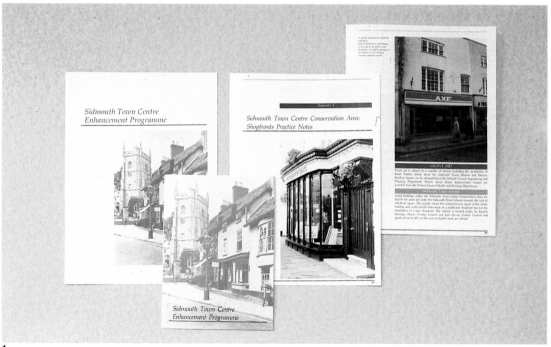

1

involvement of Road Safety Officers is very important. They will give expert advice on road safety matters and also provide valuable links with the local community particularly through their liaison with schools.

Participation

2.7 Various methods of participation and involvement can be employed to supplement formal consultation procedures. It is desirable to raise public awareness of the importance and potential of traffic calming through the dissemination of information and the mounting of publicity campaigns. This may involve meetings, exhibitions, special events, competitions, leaflets and questionnaire surveys. Media coverage needs to be encouraged.

2.8 Participation and consultation focused on individual schemes needs to take place at two key stages of the work. Firstly it is necessary to define the precise nature of the problems which the scheme is meant to address. Schemes may be more readily progressed where local traffic or environmental problems have been identified in the first instance by the local community or where successful traffic calming schemes have been implemented nearby. Secondly it will be necessary to seek views on the design proposals and to resolve any conflicts that arise. A third stage may be added to agree any final adjustments to the scheme during construction.

2.9 Where possible the views and reactions of those affected by traffic calming schemes should be sought before and after implementation. Neighbouring areas likely to be affected by such matters as the displacement of traffic should be included in the surveys.

2.10 Devon's experience ranges from one-off schemes for a particular street to comprehensive enhancement packages for important historic towns such as Dartmouth, Sidmouth, Tavistock and Totnes. In the latter cases consultation with traders and local organisations was arranged through the establishment of Steering Groups involving members of the County, District and Town Councils. These Steering Groups were supported by officer working groups who prepared environmental management plans. Member-level groups may not be necessary in every case.

2.11 Participation is more effective when members and officers make themselves available to explain the proposals and to listen to the views of local people. In the case of larger schemes temporary local information points can be established and retained until construction is complete.

2.12 It will often be helpful in promoting a scheme to show how problems have been dealt with in other towns. Attention can be drawn to examples given in documents such as this and visits can be arranged to actual schemes.

2.13 It is sometimes appropriate to seek views on two or more design options, and perhaps to implement some form of experimental scheme before final decisions are made.

2 and 3: Public
exhibitions involve the
local community in the
planning process and
help in the preparation of
the final scheme.
(Photos: Devon County
Council)

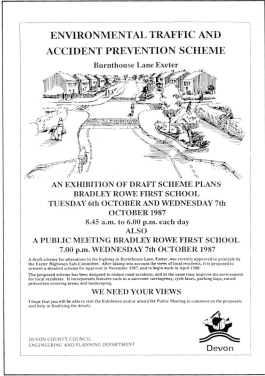

**ENVIRONMENTAL TRAFFIC AND
ACCIDENT PREVENTION SCHEME**

Burnthouse Lane Exeter

AN EXHIBITION OF DRAFT SCHEME PLANS
BRADLEY ROWE FIRST SCHOOL
TUESDAY 6th OCTOBER AND WEDNESDAY 7th
OCTOBER 1987
8.45 a.m. to 6.00 p.m. each day
ALSO
A PUBLIC MEETING BRADLEY ROWE FIRST SCHOOL
7.00 p.m. WEDNESDAY 7th OCTOBER 1987

A draft scheme for alterations to the highway in Burnthouse Lane, Exeter, was recently approved in principle by the Exeter Highways Sub-Committee. After taking into account the views of local residents, it is proposed to present a detailed scheme for approval in November 1987, and to begin work in April 1988.

The proposed scheme has been designed to reduce road accidents, and at the same time improve the environment for local residents. It incorporates features such as a narrower carriageway, cycle lanes, parking bays, raised pedestrian crossing areas, and landscaping.

WE NEED YOUR VIEWS

I hope that you will be able to visit the Exhibition and/or attend the Public Meeting to comment on the proposals and help in finalising the details.

DEVON COUNTY COUNCIL
ENGINEERING AND PLANNING DEPARTMENT

Devon

2

2.14 To be effective, participation and consultation need to be based on up-to-date information about the traffic and environmental problems in the area. Reference to accident, traffic, parking, and environmental data is important. Design proposals need to be clear, accurate and attractively presented on non-technical language. People need to be able to identify their own property on any plans displayed and to understand exactly how they will be affected by the scheme. The purpose of the consultation needs to be explicit, as should the address to which comments have to be sent and the closing date. Forms on which people can set out their views assist in collating and reporting the responses.

2.15 The involvement of the various local interests in a scheme can help in arriving at the best available solution. However where a compromise has to be made to satisfy any particular interest it is important not to undermine road safety benefits or the overall effectiveness of the scheme.

SCHEME DESIGN

2.16 It will usually be the case that traffic calming measures are accompanied by some form of environmental enhancement, and indeed traffic calming schemes are likely to be more successful and popular where the overall appearance of the street scene is improved. The types of enhancement measures which may be used are described in Section 3 of this document, and examples of good practice are illustrated in Section 4. The objective must always be to achieve an environmentally sympathetic scheme which complements the highway safety requirements and does not give rise to maintenance problems. Access requirements to individual properties need careful consideration.

2.17 In designing a scheme the needs of all groups of people have to be taken into account but particularly those with a handicap or special needs. The Institution of Highways and Transportation has prepared a set of guidelines under the title "Providing for People with a Mobility Handicap" to inform planners and engineers on the requirements of those users of highways and transport who are disabled in some way.

2.18 Particular care is needed where a scheme is designed for a Conservation Area or other area of special architectural or historic interest. It is generally appropriate to use high quality materials which are traditional to the area. The choice of materials is not only important to enhance the appearance of the area, but also to assist in defining the different functions of the various parts of the street.

2.19 Consideration should also be given to providing a design theme within particular towns or parts of towns. This approach has been followed, for example, in Totnes, Dartmouth and Sidmouth. The management plans for these towns incorporate an appropriate selection of materials, taking account of future maintenance requirements in terms of availability and cost.

2.20 It is important for developers to appreciate that they need to observe these guidelines in respect of traffic calming measures which are to be incorporated into new developments to ensure that no problems arise with regard to the roads being adopted by the Highway Authority.

2.21 In some situations traffic calming measures may need to be adjusted in the light

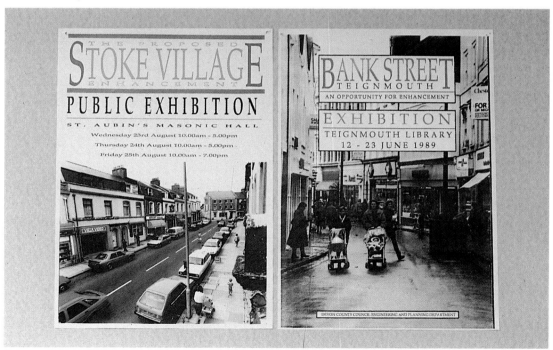

3

4: It is essential to keep the public informed on the progress of any works and to explain any new features being introduced. (Photo: Devon County Council)

of experience or where there may be a change in circumstances resulting in the particular measures no longer being the best arrangement. Consideration needs to be given to this possibility in appropriate cases at the design stage.

SCHEME CONSTRUCTION

2.22 The construction of the scheme needs to be planned and managed with the objective of ensuring the least possible disruption to the area, particularly in the case of residential, shopping and tourist areas. In the case of large schemes it may be appropriate to phase the construction works over more than one financial year, with a break in the operations during the summer periods and for Christmas. This approach was adopted successfully in Brixham with the support of local traders.

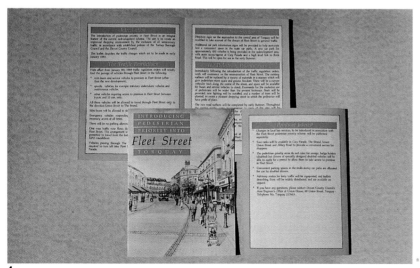

2.23 Careful supervision of contractors is needed to ensure that their operations are carried out smoothly. Any failure on the part of contractors to meet their deadlines or to minimise the disturbance to the locality reflects badly on the highway authority and the scheme.

2.24 The success of the scheme depends to a large extent on the quality of the workmanship. Careful attention to the detailing of the scheme is essential, particularly where there are changes in materials or the pattern of paving, and where street furniture is installed. A careful choice of the contractors to be included in the tender list is vital in achieving the good standard of workmanship essential to gain acceptance of the scheme by local people. The overall impression of a scheme is likely to influence people's attitudes to proposals for future schemes in their area.

MAINTENANCE

2.25 Traffic calming schemes need to be designed to minimise maintenance difficulties and costs. Attention to detail such as the avoidance of litter traps is most important. High quality design and materials can often reduce future maintenance costs as well as enhancing the appearance and popularity of schemes. Nevertheless a balance often needs to be struck between initial capital cost and ongoing maintenance costs. Future maintenance is a particular consideration when such works carried out by a developer are to be adopted on completion. Involvement of frontage property owners can be of great benefit, for example by sponsorship or contributions to particular materials or features and by encouraging them to report damage. In addition they can take the initiative in the maintenance and/or improvement of planted and landscaped areas and by the sweeping of paving fronting their property.

PROGRAMMING

2.26 Traffic calming schemes can be programmed in several ways. Firstly, a rolling programme of "stand alone" schemes should be drawn up to tackle identified problems in specified locations. Secondly, traffic calming schemes can be incorporated within programmes, such as those for housing improvements and new developments. Thirdly, the policy framework and design guidance in this document allow traffic calming measures to be implemented whenever roads and streets are being modified, repaired or re-laid. Thus opportunities for traffic calming are presented when works are carried out by Statutory Undertakers as well as highway repair and maintenance programmes. Liaison with the Statutory Undertakers is therefore vital to ensure that such opportunities are not lost.

FUNDING

2.27 Specific budget provision may be made for traffic calming schemes or they can compete in the priority lists in the usual manner. However, there are a number of other sources from which traffic calming schemes may be funded, including Transport Supplementary Grant for local safety schemes. It is important therefore that there is close liaison in the planning and design of all traffic calming, highway improvement and enhancement schemes so that the various highway programmes are complementary.

2.28 Other sources of funding include grant aid from English Heritage for certain schemes in Conservation Areas where agreed "Town Schemes" operate and contributions from District Council conservation budgets. Town Councils can often assist in the funding of, for example, street furniture. Adjoining property owners, particularly in shopping streets, may also wish to contribute to the enhancement of their own land as part of the schemes. In at least one case in Devon, a company contributed to the enhancement of a substantial area of the scheme, and sponsorship from local companies for various elements of a project is quite common. It may also be appropriate for developers to make substantial contributions or to construct schemes as part of their proposals. In cases where development would not be allowed unless associated traffic calming measures were introduced, developers would be expected to pay the full cost.

2.29 Opportunities for additional financial contributions towards a scheme should therefore be sought wherever possible, and the consultation process usually provides the best vehicle for such opportunities to be explored.

MONITORING

2.30 Monitoring of the scheme following its opening and comparisons with "before" studies are necessary to enable the highway authority to evaluate the effects of the scheme and to secure appropriate modifications where these can be achieved at a reasonable cost. However, in most cases, major changes are not likely to be practicable or cost effective. The main benefit of monitoring is to provide information which increases the highway authority's knowledge of good and bad practice in the design and implementation of traffic calming and enhancement schemes. An analysis needs to be made of the effects on surrounding areas. Monitoring can also help to ensure that the scheme is maintained to a high standard.

2.31 Monitoring is also an essential element in the procedures for both the County Council's Safety Audit and Environmental Audit and provides a check on the scheme's effectiveness in achieving safety and environmental benefits. The documents prepared by the County Council for these audits include checklists for design and maintenance engineers and planners.

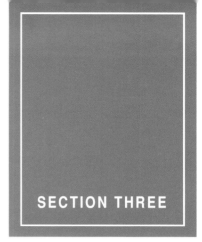

SPECIFIC MEASURES

CATEGORIES

3.1   Specific traffic calming measures fall into two main categories:-
(i) Those designed primarily to reduce vehicle speeds
(ii) Those designed to help create an environment conducive to calm driving

3.2   It is important to stress that the best results in terms of safety and the creation of a "calm" atmosphere are achieved when various measures are used in combination. As an example, the use of road humps alone is unlikely to ensure a calm driving style, or to change the character of the street in favour of its "non-traffic" activities.

3.3   Specific measures can be designed to serve multiple functions. A round top hump, for example, is mainly for speed reduction whereas a flat top hump can be integrated with the footway to provide a better pedestrian and wheelchair crossing facility.

3.4   Nineteen specific measures are described separately in the following paragraphs for ease of reference, but design teams should regard this section as a "palette" of measures which should be combined to meet scheme objectives in an attractive and effective way. Examples of the combination of various measures can be found in Section 4. The contribution of each measure and its suitability for each category of road is summarised in Table 2. Selected design guidelines or "rules of thumb" are shown in relation to each category of road in Table 3.

SUMMARY OF APPLICATIONS AND EFFECTS OF TRAFFIC CALMING MEASURES

	Speed Reduction Rating	Space Reallocation for Other Uses	Visual Enhancement of Street Scene	Suitability L	C	M	T
SPEED REDUCTION MEASURES							
3.7 Vertical Shifts in the Carriageway	A	✗	—	★	★	✚	○
3.8 Lateral Shifts in the Carriageway	B	✓	—	★	★	✚	○
3.9 Carriageway Constrictions	B	✓	✓	★	★	✚	○
3.10 Roundabouts	B	✗	✗	✚	✚	✚	✚
3.11 Small Corner Radii	B	✓	—	★	★	★	○
3.12 Priority Management	B	✗	✗	✚	✚	○	○
3.13 Road Markings	C	✗	✗	○	○	✚	★
3.14 Electronic Enforcement	C	✗	✗	○	✚	✚	✚
SUPPORTING ENVIRONMENTAL AND SAFETY MEASURES							
3.15 Optical Width	C	✗	✓	★	★	★	✚
3.16 Narrow Carriageways	C	✓	✓	★	★	★	✚
3.17 Occasional Strips	C	✓	✓	○	✚	★	✚
3.18 Surface Changes - type/colour/location	C	✗	✓	★	★	✚	○
3.19 Entrances and Gateways	C	✗	✓	★	★	✚	✚
3.20 Central Islands	C	✓	✓	○	✚	★	✚
3.21 Shared Surfaces	C	✓	✓	★	○	○	○
3.22 Footway Extensions	C	✓	✓	★	★	★	✚
3.23 Planting/Greenery	C	✗	✓	★	★	★	★
3.24 Street Furniture and Lighting	C	✗	✓	★	★	★	★
3.25 Regulations	C	✗	✗	✚	✚	★	★

KEY

SPEED REDUCTION RATING:

A   Guarantees 85 percentile traffic speeds below desired maximum
B   Reduces speeds but does not guarantee 85 percentile level
C   Serves as a reminder or encouragement to drive slowly and calmly

SUITABILITY: (FOR DIFFERENT STREET/ROAD CLASSIFICATIONS)

L	Local streets	✓ Positive effect	★ Suitable
C	Collector streets	✗ Negative effect	✚ Possible
M	Mixed priority streets	— Neutral	○ Not recommended
T	Traffic priority roads		

TABLE 2

STREET CLASSIFICATION AND SELECTED DESIGN GUIDELINES

	Classification of road (see Table 1)			
	Local	Collector	Mixed Priority	Traffic Priority
Target 85 percentile traffic speed(mph) (1)	<20	20	20/30	30/40
Self-enforcing measures required (2)	YES	YES	YES	NO
Through traffic route (3)	NO	NO	YES	YES
Target maximum traffic flow(vph) (4)	250	500	1500	N/A
Signs and road markings required (5)	NO	NO	YES	YES
Separate cycleways required (6)	NO	NO	YES	YES
Footway to continue at same level across roads (7)	YES	YES	YES	NO
Turning lanes /traffic signals appropriate (8)	NO	NO	YES	YES
Zebra and signal crossings appropriate (9)	NO	NO	YES	YES
Special bus provision appropriate (10)	NO	YES	YES	YES

EXPLANATION

1. Target speed: 85%of vehicles should travel below this speed
2. Self-enforcing measures should be taken to achieve 85 percentile level
3. Through traffic route, probably signposted
4. Target maximum flow of traffic (approximate)
5. Signs, markings, etc. are appropriate
6. Separate cycleways to be provided where possible
7. Footways preferably at continuous level in direction of main flow
8. Turning lanes and traffic light control are appropriate at key junctions
9. Zebra and light controlled pedestrian crossings are appropriate
10. Special provision may be required for buses

TABLE 3

3.5 Speed reduction measures are described in paragraphs 3.7 to 3.14 and supporting environmental and safety measures in paragraphs 3.15 to 3.25. The information for each measure is given under the following sub-headings:

- Objectives
- Speed Reduction Rating
- Design Features
- Application
- Dimensions
- Supporting Measures
- Positive Factors
- Negative Factors

SPEED REDUCTION MEASURES

3.6 Certain measures are designed primarily for speed reduction, though in most cases their application will help to meet other objectives. Speed reduction measures are rated A, B or C according to their speed reduction effectiveness (see Table 2). The rating is given on the assumption that the measure is properly designed and constructed. Faults in the design or construction of schemes may reduce their effectiveness.

Speed reduction ratings:-

A - Guarantees 85 percentile traffic speeds below desired maximum

B - Reduces speeds but does not guarantee 85 percentile level

C - Serves as a reminder or encouragement to drive slowly and calmly

Diagram 3.6.1 illustrates the expected speed reduction effects which may be achieved from measures rated A, B and C.

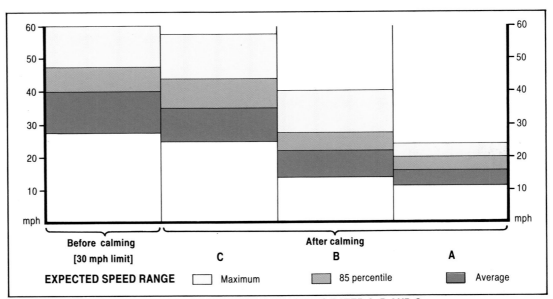

DIAGRAM 3.6.1 EXPECTED SPEED REDUCTION FROM MEASURES RATED A, B AND C.

DEFINITIONS

- Road Hump

  A raised portion of carriageway laid at right angles to the direction of traffic. Can have flat top integrated with the footway to assist crossing movements. Usually built from kerb to kerb, or tapered to retain drainage via existing channel.

- Cushion

  Raised portion of carriageway with flat top, extending over part of the carriageway width only to allow exemption for certain emergency vehicles, other large vehicles and two wheelers.

- Plateau

  In these guidelines the term plateau is used to describe a section of carriageway (from kerb to kerb) raised via ramps to footway height covering the whole of a junction.

- Ramps

  The graded or sloping sections of humps, cushions and plateaux

1

- Note: Road humps are specifically covered by The Highways (Road Humps) Regulations. Plateaux may be interpreted within the regulations as flat top humps, but cushions are not covered by regulations.

OBJECTIVES

- To improve safety by reducing vehicle speeds
- Flat top humps and plateaux can have the additional objective of allowing pedestrians and wheelchairs to cross without any change of level

SPEED REDUCTION RATING "A"

DESIGN FEATURES

Vertical shifts in the carriageway are the most effective and reliable of the speed reduction measures currently available. They may be constructed in materials different from or similar to the rest of the carriageway. A change of material may be visually useful as well as helping the speed reduction effect. Vertical shifts need to be provided at frequent intervals to ensure that any increase in speed between them is kept to a minimum. Where the carriageway is raised to footway level vertical elements such as trees and bollards may need to be provided to keep vehicles out of the pedestrian areas. Furthermore a low kerb may be required to assist people with a visual handicap. Where the road hump or plateau is constructed from kerb to kerb, satisfactory arrangements have to be made for drainage.

**1: Limited-width cushions allow buses to pass smoothly. Herne, Germany.
(Photo: T. Pharoah)**

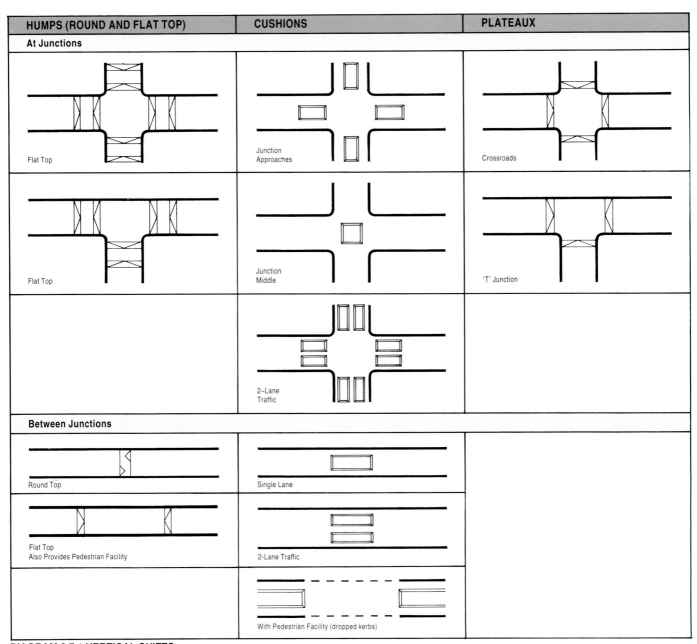

HUMPS (ROUND AND FLAT TOP)	CUSHIONS	PLATEAUX
At Junctions		
Flat Top	Junction Approaches	Crossroads
Flat Top	Junction Middle	'T' Junction
	2–Lane Traffic	
Between Junctions		
Round Top	Single Lane	
Flat Top Also Provides Pedestrian Facility	2-Lane Traffic	
	With Pedestrian Facility (dropped kerbs)	

DIAGRAM 3.7.1 VERTICAL SHIFTS

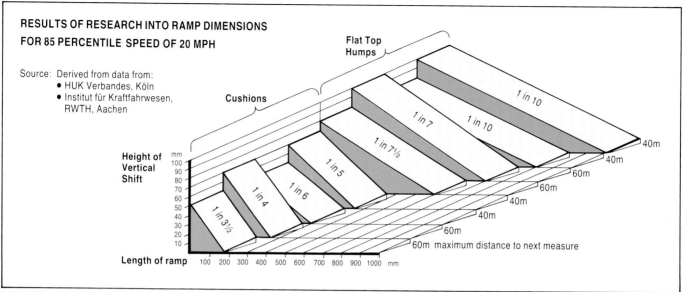

RESULTS OF RESEARCH INTO RAMP DIMENSIONS FOR 85 PERCENTILE SPEED OF 20 MPH

Source: Derived from data from:
• HUK Verbandes, Köln
• Institut für Kraftfahrwesen, RWTH, Aachen

Flat Top Humps

Cushions

Height of Vertical Shift — mm: 100 90 80 70 60 50 40 30 20 10

Length of ramp — 100 200 300 400 500 600 700 800 900 1000 mm

1 in 3½, 1 in 4, 1 in 6, 1 in 5, 1 in 7½, 1 in 7, 1 in 10, 1 in 10

40m, 40m, 60m, 60m, 40m, 40m, 60m, 60m maximum distance to next measure

DIAGRAM 3.7.2

The provision of road humps has to comply with The Highways (Road Humps) Regulations and it should be noted that road humps must be located along a road so that they are always preceded by a speed reducing feature. See also the Department of Transport Circular Roads 3/90 and Traffic Advisory Leaflet 2/90.

APPLICATION

Vertical shifts are necessary wherever excessive speed has to be prevented. They have been used mainly within "living" areas, namely in slow speed "Woonerf" type schemes, and in 20 mph zones. Shifts with less severe dimensions have been used successfully on 30 mph roads and on bus routes. Flat top humps are more useful than round top humps at places where pedestrians cross.

Cushions are easy to install and are designed not to affect certain emergency vehicles, other large vehicles and two wheelers but at the present time they are not covered by regulations.

DIMENSIONS

The dimensions and profile of the change in level of vertical shifts depend mainly on the target maximum speed and have to be chosen accordingly. For a given target speed, effectiveness depends on three factors:-
• Height of shift
• Gradient of ramp or profile of slope
• Distance between measures

2: Road humps at Duke Street, Totnes reduce speeds in a residential area. (Photo: Devon County Council)

3: Flat top humps in Burnthouse Lane, Exeter allow pedestrians to cross at a point where vehicle speeds are at their lowest. (Photo: Devon County Council)

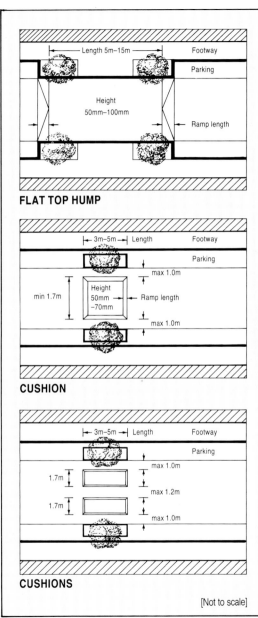

FLAT TOP HUMP

CUSHION

CUSHIONS

[Not to scale]

DIAGRAM 3.7.3 APPLICATION OF FLAT TOP HUMPS AND CUSHIONS

2

3

Diagram 3.7.2 shows the results of some research into the relationship between these three factors to achieve an 85 percentile traffic speed of 20 mph.

To achieve an 85 percentile traffic speed of 10 mph, more severe shifts are required and maximum distance between measures should be 30m.

To achieve an 85 percentile traffic speed of 30 mph (e.g. for "mixed priority" streets), less severe ramps with dimensions of 80mm or 100mm (height) by 2m or 2.5m (length) are recommended. The resulting ramp gradient of 1:25 has been found to be effective in trials in Denmark and Germany. However, Dutch guidelines recommend a more gentle ramp gradient of 1:40 with a 120mm ramp height. (It should be noted that the maximum height permitted under The Highways (Road Humps) Regulations is 100mm.)

SUPPORTING MEASURES

Vertical shifts have a poor visual effect and require combination with supporting measures to reinforce the intended driving behaviour, and to convey to drivers the "calm" atmosphere of the street. In the absence of supporting measures they may be resented by drivers and disliked by residents. Moreover, it appears that for a given target speed, vertical shifts need to be more severe when the character of the street is unchanged. Particularly effective supporting measures include carriageway narrowings and the inclusion of vertical features such as trees and street lighting.

POSITIVE FACTORS
- Best in terms of speed reduction effectiveness, including virtual elimination of "reckless" high speeds
- Easy installation which does not require repaving or reconstruction of the street
- Applicable to most street locations
- Cushions can provide exemption for certain emergency vehicles, other large vehicles and two wheelers and do not interfere with drainage

NEGATIVE FACTORS
- Vertical shifts do not by themselves contribute to change of character or environmental improvement and some designs are regarded as unsightly
- Road humps do not discriminate between classes of vehicle and can be unpopular with bus operators
- Flat top humps and plateaux need careful design for people with a visual handicap, and may require partial reconstruction of the street
- In the case of cushions high speed motorcycles could still cause problems as they are able to avoid the vertical shift

4: Lateral shift and tighter corner using re-aligned kerbing and infill planting. Zuidwolde, Netherlands.
(Photo: T. Pharoah)

OBJECTIVES
- To reduce traffic speeds and thus improve safety
- To re-arrange street space, such as parking and footways
- To interrupt long views

SPEED REDUCTION RATING "B"

DESIGN FEATURES

Speed reduction is achieved in two ways: enforced turns and limitation of drivers' forward views. Lateral shifts are created by building alternate footway extensions or islands on the carriageway. Alternate angled parking can also be used, provided that it is defined with permanent features such as planters. Forced turns using road closures are another possibility.

The shift of lateral or horizontal axis must be sufficiently severe to enforce the physical turn, or to limit the forward view, and must not be dependent on the presence or otherwise of parked vehicles.

Limiting long forward views is not normally effective as a speed reduction measure in one-way streets. In all cases, care needs to be taken to ensure that safe stopping distances are maintained.

In two-way streets, the provision of sufficient carriageway width at lateral shifts to enable vehicles to pass allows drivers to take a "racing line", and thus negates the speed reducing effect. This problem applies

4

particularly when traffic flows are below about 100 vehicles per hour, or when traffic is predominantly in one direction. The problem may be avoided by dividing the carriageway at the shift.

Layouts for collector and local roads in new developments can incorporate speed restricting bends.

APPLICATION

Lateral shifts for forced turns are appropriate for streets in "living" areas with intended speeds of 20 mph or less. They are less well suited to bus routes or routes with

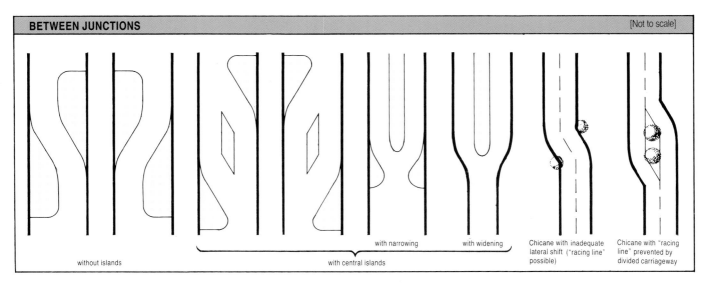

BETWEEN JUNCTIONS [Not to scale]

without islands

with central islands

with narrowing   with widening

Chicane with inadequate lateral shift ("racing line" possible)

Chicane with "racing line" prevented by divided carriageway

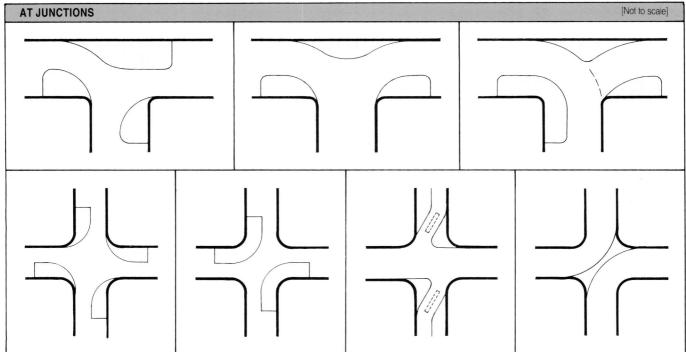

AT JUNCTIONS [Not to scaie]

DIAGRAM 3.8.1 EXAMPLES OF LATERAL SHIFTS IN THE CARRIAGEWAY

5: In shared surface areas, lateral shifts must be severe. Here children play in safety. Nijmegen, Netherlands.
(Photo: T. Pharoah)

5

significant HGV flows. They should be avoided where they might create hazards for cyclists, unless special provision is made.

Lateral shifts for limiting drivers' forward views are useful as supporting measures for speed reduction. "View blocking" helps to concentrate the driver's attention on the road immediately ahead, while long views are unnecessary in slow speed areas. Lateral shifts for this purpose do not need to be severe.

Lateral shifts on 30 mph roads are useful mainly for limiting long forward views or for purposes other than speed reduction, such as the reallocation of carriageway space.

DIMENSIONS

To produce an effective "forced turn", the lateral shift in the carriageway needs to be no less than the width of a traffic lane. Drivers should be required to make a turn of at least 45 degrees. Narrow carriageway widths are generally required and possible dimensions are given below. However, each case will need to be subject to the consultations detailed in Section 2.
• One way traffic - 3.0m to 3.6m
• Two way traffic - 4.5m to 6.5m

SUPPORTING MEASURES

Vertical shifts may be necessary to ensure adequate speed reduction. Planting is desirable to lessen the impact of islands, build-outs, etc., to reduce visual dominance of parked cars, and to limit the forward view. A high standard of street lighting is required.

POSITIVE FACTORS
- Can be cheap and simple to construct if no rebuilding of the carriageway is required
- May avoid need for vertical shifts
- Alternate parking reduces pedestrian danger by providing unobstructed view of 50 % of footway
- Can allow interesting street design features

NEGATIVE FACTORS
- Can radically alter and sometimes spoil the linear character of the street
- Difficult to achieve good speed reduction effect whilst allowing access for larger vehicles
- Can be uncomfortable for bus passengers
- Can be hazardous for cyclists if speeds are higher than about 15 mph

6

6: Granite setts following the curved wall of a church mark out a lateral shift, and thus emphasize an attractive feature of the street. Nuremburg, Germany. (Photo: T. Pharoah)

8: Through road narrowed where a pedestrian zone crosses. Buses get priority entry to the narrowed section. Bergisch Gladbach, Germany. (Photo: T. Pharoah)

7

3.9 CARRIAGEWAY CONSTRICTIONS

(SEE ALSO FOOTWAY EXTENSIONS)

OBJECTIVES

• To limit the ability of vehicles to pass one another, and thus to limit speeds and/or to interrupt traffic flow
• To limit overtaking
• To reduce pedestrian crossing distance
• To restrict the size of vehicle
• To provide priority for buses
• To prevent on-street parking
• To define or shelter on-street parking spaces

SPEED REDUCTION RATING "B"

In some circumstances speed reduction can be good, but the effect is unreliable and dependent on traffic conditions, e.g. when cars have to proceed behind cyclists, or give way to oncoming traffic.

DESIGN FEATURES

Constrictions are "spot" measures at intervals along the street (e.g. at vertical shifts or at junctions). They can be achieved on one or both sides of the road, or by the inclusion of a central island (see Diagram 3.9.1). Constrictions will have different effects and design requirements in one-way and two-way streets. They are an important feature of multi-objective traffic calming design, but need to be combined with other measures for effective speed reduction.

APPLICATION

Constrictions are useful in both "living" and "mixed priority" areas where traffic volumes are less than 500 vehicles per hour. They are suitable for one-way and two-way streets and useful in association with prohibitions relating to large vehicles.

8

DIMENSIONS

Width is influenced by various factors including:-

- One-way or two-way traffic
- Traffic volume
- Bicycle/vehicle mix
- Separate cycle provision
- Provision for buses
- HGV prohibition

SUGGESTED WIDTHS OF CONSTRICTIONS

TWO-WAY TRAFFIC (<500 VEHICLES PER HOUR)

Local streets (no passing, parking) -3.0m to 3.6m
Collector streets - 4.0m
Mixed priority (occasional HGV) - 4.5m
Traffic priority streets - not suitable

ONE-WAY TRAFFIC (ANY VOLUME)

All streets (single lane only) - 3.0m
HGV prohibition (single lane only) - 2.0m to 2.1m

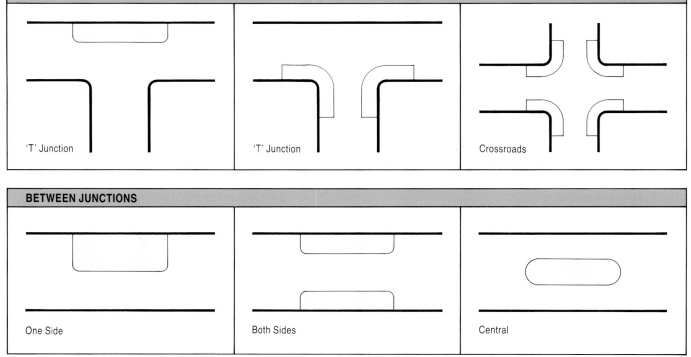

AT JUNCTIONS

'T' Junction

'T' Junction

Crossroads

BETWEEN JUNCTIONS

One Side

Both Sides

Central

DIAGRAM 3.9.1 CARRIAGEWAY CONSTRICTIONS

9

10

9: Constriction with separate cycle "gates". Camden, London. (Photo: T. Pharoah)

10: Concrete bollards and raised planters reinforce this constriction in Church Road, Exeter. (Photo: Devon County Council)

SUPPORTING MEASURES

Planting and other vertical features are required. To ensure reliable speed reduction constrictions may need to be combined with vertical or lateral shifts. Specific provision for cyclists may be necessary in some cases.

POSITIVE FACTORS

- Useful speed reduction in some circumstances, and positive contribution to several traffic calming objectives
- Assists pedestrians crossing the road
- An important supporting measure for other speed reduction measures

NEGATIVE FACTORS

- Not always reliable as a "stand alone" speed reduction device
- Can cause problems for cyclists if specific provision is not made

OBJECTIVES
- Speed reduction
- Smoothing traffic flow and reducing vehicle conflicts

SPEED REDUCTION RATING "B"

Rating is in comparison with previously unimpeded speed (e.g. as at a priority intersection).

DESIGN FEATURES

Speed reduction results from the creation of a lateral shift in the carriageway, and priority to traffic from the off-side. Visual appearance in sensitive environments needs careful consideration. The surround to the central island of a small roundabout can be hardened to allow overrun by large vehicles.

12

11

11: Roundabouts can be useful at more important junctions, but pedestrians and cyclists need special consideration. Oer Erckenschwick, Germany. (Photo: T. Pharoah)

12: Roundabouts can cause discomfort for bus passengers. Rennes, France. (Photo: T. Pharoah)

APPLICATION

The design and appearance of conventional roundabouts tends to limit their use to "traffic" areas where they can reduce accidents and smooth traffic flow. Mini roundabouts are often used on distributor and collector roads within residential areas. They may be useful in 20 mph zones where there are low volumes of pedestrians and cyclists.

DIMENSIONS

Advice on the design and dimensions of roundabouts is given in "Roads and Traffic in Urban Areas" (page 339). Within 20 mph streets, multi-lane roundabouts are inappropriate.

SUPPORTING MEASURES

The design should incorporate planting and other features to soften the appearance. Separate provision for pedestrians and cyclists is usually required. Further speed reduction measures may be required in 20 mph areas.

13: A ramped area around the central island can reduce speeds while allowing occasional long vehicles to "trail" over it. Here the area is paved with granite and marked by a 25mm kerb upstand. A working antique lighting column stands in the island as a feature only. Sheffield. (Photo: K. Platt)

13

POSITIVE FACTORS

- Smooth flow of traffic (less braking and acceleration) where traffic flows are moderate
- All turning movements possible
- Properly designed they will reduce traffic speeds and alert drivers to their surroundings

NEGATIVE FACTORS

- Relatively high space requirements
- Danger and/or inconvenience for pedestrians and cyclists
- Uncomfortable for bus passengers
- Often considered unsightly

OBJECTIVES

- To slow turning movements at junctions to assist pedestrians when crossing, and to provide greater safety for cyclists (see Diagram 3.11.1)

SPEED REDUCTION RATING "B"

Rating "B" for turning movements only.

DESIGN FEATURES

The design should be appropriate to the classification of the streets involved. Ramped corners can be used to slow cars while still allowing access by large vehicles.

APPLICATION

Useful at all junctions within "living" and "mixed priority" areas where turning movements would otherwise be too fast. Small radii are not necessary where slow speeds are achieved by other means, or where the footway is set away from the corner.

DIMENSIONS

Suggested maximum kerb radii (m) if footways and corners are adjacent.

Road class	Local	Collector	Mixed
Local	2		
Collector	2	3	
Mixed	3	4	6
Traffic	4	6	8

14

15

14: Excessive corner radii encourage speeding and are hazardous for pedestrians. (Photo: T. Pharoah)

15: Small radii at corners allow pedestrians to cross conveniently. In this example, dropped kerbs are also provided. Battersea, London. (Photo: T. Pharoah)

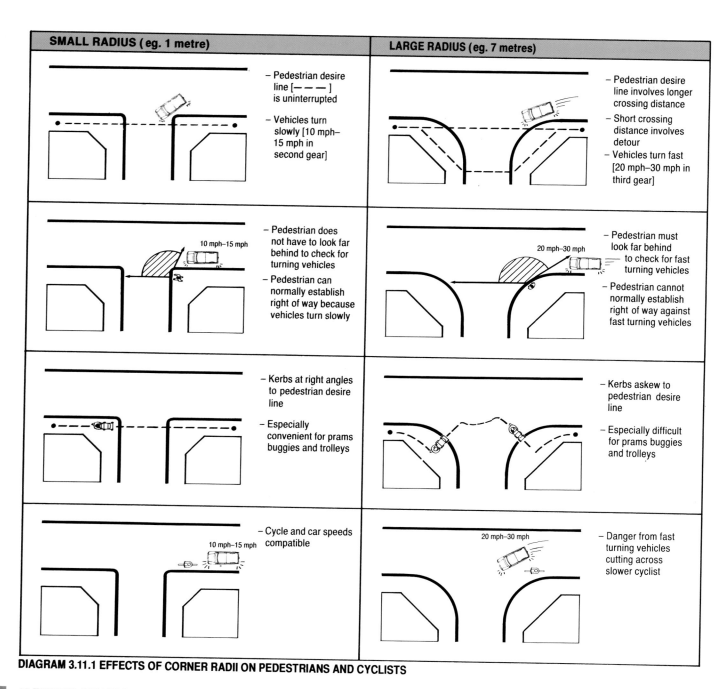

SMALL RADIUS (eg. 1 metre)	LARGE RADIUS (eg. 7 metres)

SMALL RADIUS (eg. 1 metre)

– Pedestrian desire line [– – –] is uninterrupted

– Vehicles turn slowly [10 mph–15 mph in second gear]

– Pedestrian does not have to look far behind to check for turning vehicles

– Pedestrian can normally establish right of way because vehicles turn slowly

– Kerbs at right angles to pedestrian desire line

– Especially convenient for prams buggies and trolleys

– Cycle and car speeds compatible

LARGE RADIUS (eg. 7 metres)

– Pedestrian desire line involves longer crossing distance

– Short crossing distance involves detour

– Vehicles turn fast [20 mph–30 mph in third gear]

– Pedestrian must look far behind to check for fast turning vehicles

– Pedestrian cannot normally establish right of way against fast turning vehicles

– Kerbs askew to pedestrian desire line

– Especially difficult for prams buggies and trolleys

– Danger from fast turning vehicles cutting across slower cyclist

DIAGRAM 3.11.1 EFFECTS OF CORNER RADII ON PEDESTRIANS AND CYCLISTS

SUPPORTING MEASURES

Bollards can prevent overrunning of footway at corners. Dimensions can be relaxed if speeds are slowed by ramped junctions or other means. Ramped corners may be appropriate in "mixed priority" and "traffic" areas. Central islands may be needed in mouth of junction to prevent vehicles taking a "racing line".

POSITIVE FACTORS

- Helps pedestrians to establish right of way over turning vehicles at junctions
- Easier to ensure that footway meets carriageway at 90 degrees at junctions
- Reduces danger of cyclists being "cut across" by turning vehicles

NEGATIVE FACTORS

- More difficult access for large vehicles limits radii reduction in some circumstances

16

17

16/17: Large corner radii cause particular inconvenience for people with prams, wheelchairs, etc. (Photos: T. Pharoah)

3.12 PRIORITY MANAGEMENT

OBJECTIVES

- Speed reduction, to change priorities and to introduce "give ways"

SPEED REDUCTION RATING "B"

DESIGN FEATURES

Alignment of the carriageway can help to convey and enforce priority rules. Priority may be changed from one road to another. In exceptional circumstances, priority may be changed to traffic approaching from the nearside or removed altogether. When a roundabout is constructed priority from the offside is usually established.

APPLICATION

Other than the conventional use of roundabouts, these measures have not been introduced in the UK and are probably only suitable for experimental use in 20 mph zones for the time being.

DIMENSIONS

Does not apply.

SUPPORTING MEASURES

Physical measures such as constrictions required to reinforce the priority arrangements.

POSITIVE AND NEGATIVE FACTORS

- Not known in UK in this context.

OBJECTIVES

- To guide drivers and to improve predictability of vehicle path for the benefit of pedestrians and cyclists
- To indicate priority

SPEED REDUCTION RATING "C"

DESIGN FEATURES

Subject to regulations and guidance from the Department of Transport.

APPLICATION

Useful in "traffic" areas for safety, and may be extended into "mixed priority" areas for the same reason. To be avoided as far as possible in "living" areas with a speed limit of 20 mph or below.

DIMENSIONS

As laid down by regulations or specifically authorised by the Department of Transport.

SUPPORTING MEASURES

Not applicable.

POSITIVE FACTORS

- Simple, cheap and usually effective
- Useful at night

NEGATIVE FACTORS

- Unsightly, and lack self-enforcing qualities

18

19

20

18: Unsightly bus stop markings, Germany. (Photo: T. Pharoah)

19: Signs and markings are noticeable by their absence in this traffic-calmed street. Cologne, Germany. (Photo: T. Pharoah)

20: These markings clearly indicate the cycle path at the approach to traffic lights in Exeter. (Photo: Devon County Council)

- Some markings (e.g. centre lines) encourage speed

3.14 ELECTRONIC ENFORCEMENT

OBJECTIVES

- Speed reduction
- Compliance with traffic law

SPEED REDUCTION RATING "C"

DESIGN FEATURES

Electronic equipment can be linked to warning lights, signs and photographic recording equipment.

Signs on their own can be counter-productive as some motorists like to activate them, but they could be backed up with a "Gatso" type photographic camera. A sign could give the message "reduce speed now", "police speed check ahead", "driving too fast", etc.

APPLICATION

Electronic enforcement may be applied at locations where speeding vehicles could be a problem (e.g. at school or hospital entrances) and where other physical measures are inappropriate. They are suitable in "traffic" and "mixed priority" areas only.

DIMENSIONS

Not applicable.

SUPPORTING MEASURES

Physical measures may help to ensure effectiveness. Central islands in particular eliminate overtaking where such measures are located.

POSITIVE FACTORS

- Alerts drivers and assists with enforcement

NEGATIVE FACTORS

- Police follow-up of offenders is required
- Can add to street clutter

SUPPORTING ENVIRONMENTAL AND SAFETY MEASURES

The following measures have a Speed Reduction Rating of "C" or less, and are recommended for use in combination with higher rated speed reduction measures.

3.15 OPTICAL WIDTH

OBJECTIVES

• To encourage slow driving and to enhance street character

DESIGN FEATURES

Drivers' perception of the appropriate driving speed is influenced by the relationship between the width of the street and the height of vertical elements. It can be shown that speeds are lower where the height of vertical features is greater than the width of the street. This effect can be created by a combination of carriageway narrowing and the introduction of adjacent trees or other vertical features as shown in Diagram 3.15.1.

APPLICATION

Suitable where the street has an "open" or broad aspect which encourages speeding. Suitable for both links and junctions (see 3.19).

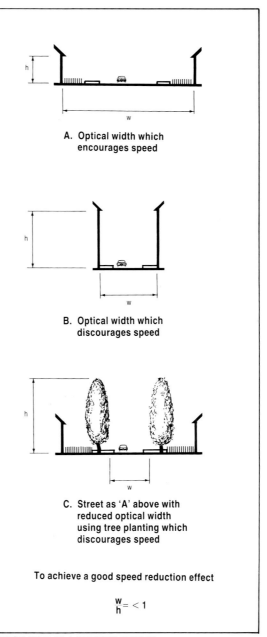

A. Optical width which encourages speed

B. Optical width which discourages speed

C. Street as 'A' above with reduced optical width using tree planting which discourages speed

To achieve a good speed reduction effect

$$\frac{w}{h} = < 1$$

DIAGRAM 3.15.1 OPTICAL WIDTH

21

22

23

21: The "optical width" of the street can be reduced with tree planting, as in this otherwise wide Berlin street. Berlin, Germany. (Photo: T. Pharoah)

22: "Optical width" influences traffic speed. Wide streets with long, open views encourage speeding. (Photo: T. Pharoah)

23: Where the height of vertical features exceeds the street width, speeds are moderated. Herne, Germany. (Photo: T. Pharoah)

DIMENSIONS

Speed reduction can be significant when the height of buildings (or other adjacent features) exceeds the width of the street.

SUPPORTING MEASURES

Physical speed reduction measures such as humps or lateral shifts are also required.

POSITIVE FACTORS

• If trees are used there will normally be other benefits such as improved street appearance and micro-climate

NEGATIVE FACTORS

• When trees are used the effects may be reduced in winter when they are without foliage

OBJECTIVES

- To emphasize low speed and priority to pedestrians and cyclists
- To discourage overtaking
- To reduce the width of carriageway which pedestrians have to cross
- To create space for non-traffic activities
- To reduce "optical width" (see 3.15)
- To provide defined on-street parking and loading space

DESIGN FEATURES

Although wide carriageways tend to encourage speeding, reducing carriageway width is not a reliable or sufficient speed reduction measure in urban streets. Nevertheless, if speeds are reduced by other means, then carriageways can usually be reduced in width thus releasing space for other purposes. Access requirements to individual properties need careful consideration. In most urban streets, large vehicles account for a very small proportion of traffic and need not therefore dictate the overall layout.

24: A main traffic street reduces from four lanes to two, making crossing easier for pedestrians. Textured paving is used to help those with a visual handicap at the approach to dropped kerbs. Camden, London. (Photo: T.Pharoah)

25: Narrow carriageways are sufficient in quiet residential streets. Here this has been achieved by the use of tree planting in the former carriageway to define parking bays. Nijmegen, Netherlands. (Photo: T. Pharoah)

26: Dual carriageway with parking lane, "shared" cycle lane, and narrow driving lane. Large vehicles cannot pass cyclists, so traffic is usually slowed to the pace of cyclists. Outer ring road, Eindhoven, Netherlands. (Photo: T. Pharoah)

24

25

26

20 mph STREETS		30 mph STREETS	
One-Way ≤ 1000 vph HGV/Bus ≤ 5% Cycles Cat: L C M	3.25m	One-Way Any volume HGV/Bus ≤ 10% Cycles separate Cat: M	3.25m
Two-Way ≤ 500 vph HGV/Bus ≤ 5% Cycles Cat: L	4.5m	One-Way ≥ 500 vph HGV/Bus ≤ 10% Cycles Cat: M T	4.0m
Two-Way 500-1000 vph HGV/Bus ≤ 5% Cycles Cat: C M	5.0m	Two-Way ≤ 1000 vph HGV/Bus ≤ 5% Cycles separate Cat: M	5.5m
Two-Way 500-1000 vph HGV/Bus ≤ 10% Cycles separate Cat: C M	5.5m	Two-Way ≥ 1000 vph HGV/Bus ≤ 5% Cycles separate Cat: M T	6.5m
Two-Way 500-1000 vph HGV/Bus ≤ 10% Cycles Cat: C M	6.5m	Two-Way ≥ 1000 vph HGV/Bus (any percentage) Cycles Cat: M T	7.3m

KEY: L Local streets   C Collector streets   M Mixed priority streets   T Traffic priority roads

DIAGRAM 3.16.1 CARRIAGEWAY WIDTHS IN TRAFFIC CALMED STREETS

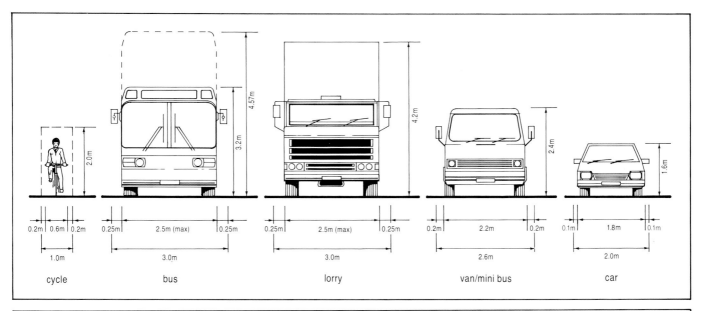

Space for passing

20 mph areas	Between cycles – motor vehicles	0.4m	30 mph areas	Between all vehicles	0.75m–1.0m
	Between motor vehicles	0.25m–0.3m			

DIAGRAM 3.16.2 BASIC DIMENSIONS FOR DETERMINING CARRIAGEWAY WIDTH

APPLICATION

Excessive carriageway width is best avoided on all roads in built-up areas, but narrow carriageways are especially valuable where extra space is required for pedestrians, cyclists and for frontage activities.

DIMENSIONS

Carriageway width and layout should be determined by a range of factors. Key factors will be the road classification and intended speed, the presence or otherwise of cycles, lorries and buses, traffic volume, visual appearance and environment. Widths can be further reduced when "occasional strips" are used (see 3.17). Appropriate dimensions are set out in Diagrams 3.16.1 and 3.16.2.

SUPPORTING MEASURES

Narrow carriageways benefit from combination with measures to reduce optical width (see 3.15) and to interrupt long views (see 3.8).

POSITIVE FACTORS

- Applicable to all urban roads
- Allows reclamation of space for other uses

NEGATIVE FACTORS

- Potential for conflict between motor vehicles and cyclists, unless separate provision is made for the latter
- Reduced width when a vehicle breaks down and for certain maintenance operations

OBJECTIVES

- To allow reduction of carriageway width (see 3.16) while retaining access for buses and lorries
- To improve the optical effect for slow driving
- To provide greater safety for pedestrians crossing the street, for cyclists, and for on-street parking/loading activity

These various objectives are illustrated in Diagram 3.17.1.

27

DESIGN FEATURES

Occasional strips are set out adjacent to and at the same level as the main carriageway. They occur either side of the

27: Occasional strips either side of a narrow carriageway have multiple uses. Cars stay on the main carriageway, but lorries must use the full width to pass. People parking gain useful protection, and pedestrians can be seen more easily when waiting to cross. Hennef, Germany. (Photo: T. Pharoah)

28: Informal side strips can enhance the appearance of village streets. Here the strips are in sympathy with the informal arrangement of buildings and side accessways. Borgentreich, Germany. (Photo: T. Pharoah)

28

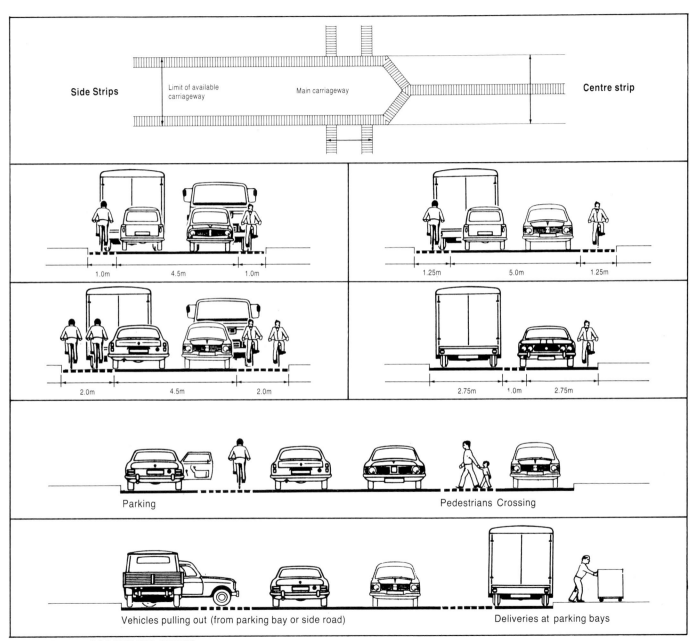

Side Strips

Limit of available
carriageway

Main carriageway

Centre strip

1.0m 4.5m 1.0m

1.25m 5.0m 1.25m

2.0m 4.5m 2.0m

2.75m 1.0m 2.75m

Parking

Pedestrians Crossing

Vehicles pulling out (from parking bay or side road)

Deliveries at parking bays

DIAGRAM 3.17.1 OCCASIONAL STRIPS

29

30

29: Occasional strips can also be provided in the centre of a narrow carriageway, to provide safer crossing for pedestrians and safer turning for vehicles. Hennef, Germany. (Photo: T. Pharoah)

30: Side strips help to reduce the "optical width" of the street and allow buses into an otherwise narrow street. Recklinghausen, Germany. (Photo: T. Pharoah)

carriageway, and may also be used to divide the carriageway. They are distinguished from the main carriageway by the use of surfaces with a different texture or colour. Textures should not be so rough as to discourage cyclists, unless separate cycleways are provided.

APPLICATION

Particularly well suited to 20 mph "collector" roads and 20 mph or 30 mph "mixed priority" roads, including village through roads.

DIMENSIONS

The width of occasional strips will depend on their purpose in each location. Side strips of between 0.75m and 1.25m accommodate the difference in width between a car and a lorry, which is the main purpose, but wider strips can be used. Narrow strips of 0.25m to 0.5m may help pedestrians and parking activity but are less likely to benefit cyclists (see Diagram 3.17.1).

SUPPORTING MEASURES

Raised islands or features such as lamp standards may be helpful to pedestrians where central strips of sufficient width are used.

POSITIVE FACTORS

- Can reinforce speed reduction and other traffic calming objectives while retaining access for moderate volumes of larger vehicles
- Provides greater functional and design flexibility especially where street width is limited, as in historic towns and villages for example

NEGATIVE FACTORS

- Probably unsuitable where larger vehicles form a high proportion of traffic
- Textured surfaces may discourage their use by cyclists

3.18 SURFACE CHANGES
TYPE/COLOUR/LOCATION

OBJECTIVES

- To distinguish between different surface functions (e.g. see 3.17)
- To improve street appearance
- To reinforce speed reduction measures
- To simplify construction of traffic calming measures in the carriageway
- To improve visual impact, particularly in poor light and under street lighting

DESIGN FEATURES

Texture changes which result in a rougher carriageway surface can produce a rumble to alert drivers to their surroundings. Where rough textures are used for the carriageway, smooth surfaces should be provided where footways and cycleways cross. Materials should be chosen according to the existing street character, especially in places of townscape merit. Consideration must be given to changes in skid resistance. Different colours can be used for specific purposes, e.g. a red slurry for cycleways. However, the effects of coloured surfaces may vary under different lighting conditions or when wet. Paved surfaces, including

31

32

32: The use of red slurry seal clearly defines this section of the Exe Cycle Route. (Photo: Devon County Council)

33: Safety margins between carriageway and bollards here become a positive feature with granite banding. Red paving distinguishes a cycle path through the pedestrian area. Cologne, Germany. (Photo: T. Pharoah)

kerbs and borders, need to be carefully designed and constructed, if possible using large-scale plans (e.g. 1:100 or 1:20).

APPLICATION

Textured surfacing may be useful wherever visual or sensory reinforcement of surface function is required. It is often used to define a ramped entrance into a side road, and may also be used for decorative purposes. It is not recommended where traffic speeds are higher than 30 mph.

DIMENSIONS

Not applicable.

SUPPORTING MEASURES

Should be integrated with other design elements.

33

34: Traditional high-quality paving can still be found in many historic areas. Here, iron railings throw a pattern of light across real stone paving, and a cobbled gutter banded with granite. Lichfield. (Photo: T. Pharoah)

35: Attention to detail can produce attractive results. The bollards here, for example, are specifically positioned in the granite banding to avoid the need to cut paving tiles. Cologne, Germany. (Photo: T. Pharoah)

34

35

POSITIVE FACTORS
- Can create visual interest and improved street appearance
- Some speed reduction effect, especially when combined with vertical shifts
- A clear contrast can be provided for different intended uses of the available space

NEGATIVE FACTORS
- Rough surfaces such as granite setts are noisy at speeds above about 15 mph, and thus may be unsuitable where people live nearby
- Rough surfaces are potentially hazardous for cyclists and pedestrians
- Paving can be less comfortable for cyclists than asphalt

OBJECTIVES

• To mark the beginning and end of areas where different rules or expectations for drivers apply, or where special functions occur

DESIGN FEATURES

The "gateway" effect can be achieved by the use of vertical features either side of and close to the carriageway, or particularly by the use of some form of archway. Archways can be created simply by providing wires across the street for climbing plants, or by the use of more elaborate structures. Some design possibilities are illustrated in Diagram 3.19.1.

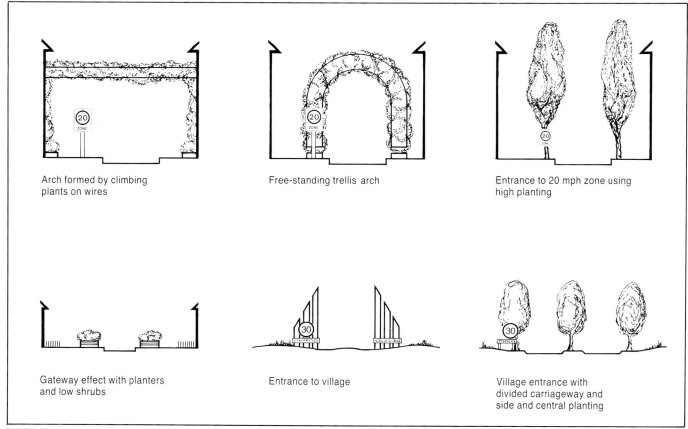

Arch formed by climbing plants on wires

Free-standing trellis arch

Entrance to 20 mph zone using high planting

Gateway effect with planters and low shrubs

Entrance to village

Village entrance with divided carriageway and side and central planting

DIAGRAM 3.19.1 ENTRANCES AND GATEWAYS

36

37

36: A village entrance is here given emphasis with "gateposts", nameboard and a change in surfacing. Zuidlaren, Netherlands.
(Photo: T. Pharoah)

37: An archway makes a grand entrance to this quiet Kensington mews, London.
(Photo: T. Pharoah)

APPLICATION

Entrances to slow speed or 20 mph zones, villages and special areas such as street markets, historic centres.

DIMENSIONS

The gateway width needs to have regard for any clearance requirements due to vertical features adjacent to the carriageway. The minimum height (clearance) should be 5.01m or 4.25m if buses and lorries are excluded.

SUPPORTING MEASURES

Gateways usually need to coincide with carriageway constrictions, to reinforce the visual effect, and to avoid over-large dimensions.

POSITIVE FACTORS

- Important effect on drivers' perception of change of street priorities
- Can add visual interest to the streetscape

NEGATIVE FACTORS

- Structures may be too large for the scale of the street if all classes of vehicle are allowed through

OBJECTIVES

- To make crossing easier and safer for pedestrians
- To interrupt forward views (see 3.8)
- To reduce the optical width of the street (see 3.15)
- To reduce carriageway width (see 3.9 and 3.16)
- To assist in the creation of gateways (see 3.19)
- To provide separate lanes for turning traffic and/or shelter for turning traffic
- To prevent overtaking

Some design possibilities are illustrated in Diagram 3.20.1.

DESIGN FEATURES

Islands usually need to be raised above carriageway level (e.g. using kerbs), but where pedestrians are to cross there need to be level areas flush with the carriageway. Lamp posts, bollards, etc. should not obstruct these level areas. Islands of appropriate size can enhance street appearance if well designed and landscaped.

Internally illuminated bollards may need to be placed at each end of islands with an illuminated beacon near the centre if appropriate. Islands sited directly opposite bus stops can help to slow the traffic and retain priority for buses, providing other traffic is not subjected to undue delay.

38

APPLICATION

Most useful in two-way streets with moderate or heavy traffic, and where pedestrians require frequent crossing opportunities such as in shopping streets and village centres. Not usually required in lightly trafficked streets, except to create constrictions or for environmental enhancement. Also useful at entrances to villages.

38: Central islands can be used to narrow carriageways, but separate provision for cyclists may be needed, as in this example. Herne, Germany. (Photo: T. Pharoah)

39: A central island together with kerb extensions and tree planting reduce the optical width of this street in Auckland, New Zealand. (Photo: Tim Hipwell)

39

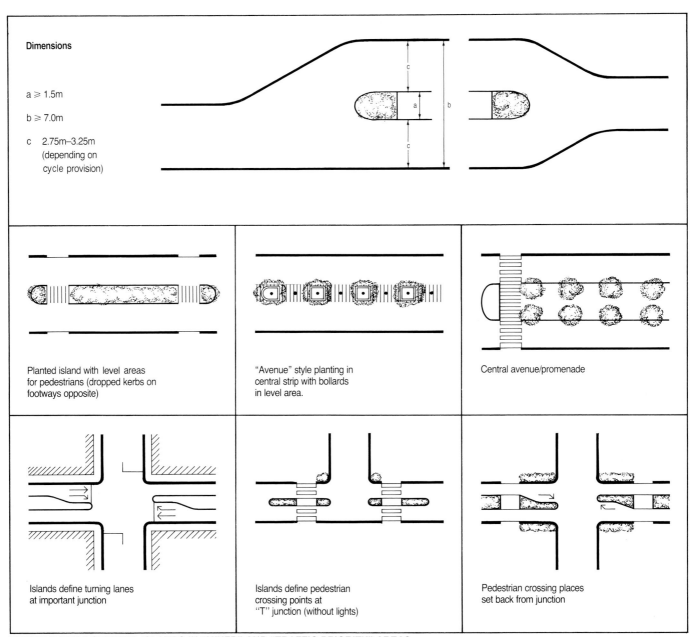

Dimensions

a ⩾ 1.5m

b ⩾ 7.0m

c 2.75m–3.25m
(depending on
cycle provision)

Planted island with level areas
for pedestrians (dropped kerbs on
footways opposite)

"Avenue" style planting in
central strip with bollards
in level area.

Central avenue/promenade

Islands define turning lanes
at important junction

Islands define pedestrian
crossing points at
"T" junction (without lights)

Pedestrian crossing places
set back from junction

DIAGRAM 3.20.1 CENTRAL ISLANDS IN "MIXED" AND "TRAFFIC PRIORITY" AREAS

DIMENSIONS

Islands should be at least 2m wide and about 4m long if tree planting is to be included. Level areas where pedestrians are encouraged to cross should be of generous length, and in the case of long central islands should be repeated at frequent intervals, especially in shopping streets.

SUPPORTING MEASURES

Not applicable.

POSITIVE FACTORS

- Provides safety and convenience for pedestrians while contributing to other speed reduction and environmental objectives

NEGATIVE FACTORS

- Reduces space at each side of the street (for a given carriageway width)

40

40: Central islands can allow pedestrians to cross in greater safety, and can be planted to create an attractive feature. Langenfeld, Germany.
(Photo: T. Pharoah)

41: Unless properly designed and regulated, shared spaces can become chaotic and unsightly parking lots. In this example parked cars create hazards and inconvenience for pedestrians. Cologne, Germany.
(Photo: T. Pharoah)

42: Shared surface "Woonerf" with spaces defined by mature trees and shrubs. Note the short forward views and severe lateral shift to ensure slow speeds. Nijmegen, Netherlands.
(Photo: T. Pharoah)

3.21 SHARED SURFACES

41

OBJECTIVES

• To allow pedestrians freedom of movement within the street

DESIGN FEATURES

Pedestrian freedom to use the entire street surface in safety can only be achieved if vehicle volumes are relatively low, and speeds are kept to "running pace". These requirements dictate the circumstances in which shared surfaces are appropriate, and also determine the design elements. In particular, very low vehicle speeds need to be self enforcing through the use of lateral shifts, ramps, etc.

42

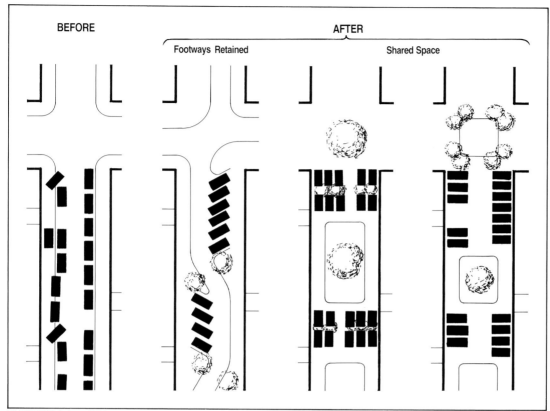

BEFORE

AFTER

Footways Retained

Shared Space

DIAGRAM 3.21.1 EXAMPLE OF SHARED SURFACE LAYOUTS

In original shared surface schemes (such as the Dutch "Woonerf") no demarcation was allowed between footway and carriageway. This can, however, lead to feelings of insecurity for pedestrians and especially people with a visual handicap. Some demarcation may often be desirable, and can be achieved without compromising the "precinct" objective. As an example, bollards or low kerbs can be used, while street furniture can be placed in such a way as to separate areas where people walk from where vehicles pass.

Parking should be in identified bays. In the Netherlands, parking is permitted only in bays identified with a letter "P", but there are currently no comparable traffic regulations for shared surfaces in the UK.

Vehicles have to be kept away from doorways. Care needs to be taken to prevent the precinct becoming a "rat run" for two-wheelers.

43: In shared spaces, those with a visual handicap in particular can feel insecure. Here, vehicle space is defined by a low kerb to help them. Bad Godesburg, Germany.
(Photo: T. Pharoah)

44: Shared space solution applied in a shopping area. Note the defined parking bays (served by a single, multiple parking meter to reduce clutter). Buses also use this street. The Hague, Netherlands.
(Photo: T. Pharoah)

APPLICATION

Shared surfaces are suited to local streets with no through traffic and where traffic flow is no more than about 300 vehicles per hour, so that pedestrians can benefit from being able to cross from side to side frequently and in any place. They function best where there is intensive pedestrian activity and where traffic flow is less than 100 vehicles per hour. They can be applied to junctions and links.

Intensive pedestrian activity may occur where there are shops on both sides of the street, outside railway stations, at hospital or college entrances, etc. High density housing areas may also generate intensive pedestrian

43

activity, especially if there are no off-street play areas for children.

Shared surface solutions are now used sparingly in some countries.

44

BEFORE

AFTER

BEFORE

DIAGRAM 3.21.2 SHARED SPACE, BEFORE AND AFTER

AFTER

45: A traditional "shared space access road", perhaps better known as a "Mews". Such mixed use areas function well if the volume of parked and moving vehicles is small. Kensington, London.
(Photo: T. Pharoah)

46: A pedestrianised area of Plymouth still allows limited servicing of banks and shops.
(Photo: Devon County Council)

47: Modern housing area incorporating "Woonerf" shared spaces. Delft, Netherlands.
(Photo: T. Pharoah)

45

46

47

DIMENSIONS

The space should not be so large as to allow the presence of parked or moving vehicles to dominate the street scene. The distance between speed reducing elements should not be greater than about 30m. No part of a precinct should be more than about 300m-400m from a "normal" road. In some countries shared surface precincts must not join directly onto roads with speed limits higher than 30 mph.

SUPPORTING MEASURES

The design needs to include planting, paving, street furniture and other elements to create a "precinct" atmosphere.

POSITIVE FACTORS

• Well-designed schemes in appropriate locations have proved their popularity with residents and shoppers, and have the ability to provide safe and convenient conditions for all road users

NEGATIVE FACTORS

• Can be expensive to provide
• Unless properly designed and regulated, can become a chaotic and unsightly parking lot
• Pedestrians, especially those with a visual handicap, can feel insecure unless areas free from vehicles are retained.

OBJECTIVES

- To provide more space for pedestrians and reduce carriageway crossing distances
- To prevent parking at or near junctions, pedestrian crossings and bus stops and to shelter and define permitted parking areas
- To improve the visibility of pedestrians at junctions, crossings and bus stops

DESIGN FEATURES

The design of footway extensions should be integrated with existing footways, for example by using the same paving materials, and by maintaining the same level. The enlarged area should not be cut across by surface drainage channels. Extensions at corners should be designed to avoid the problems for pedestrians created by large kerb radii (see 3.11). Extensions should where possible be large enough to define on-street parking areas. Consideration should be given to the creation of "staying space" where people can stop to rest, chat, enjoy the scene, etc. Such space is appreciated at focal points for pedestrian activity such as outside churches, libraries and other community buildings, and in all shopping areas. Particular attention needs to be paid to the requirements of cyclists. Some design possibilities are shown in Diagram 3.22.1.

48

49

48: Simple footway extensions discourage dangerous parking at corners, though bollards or other means are also needed if parking demand is high. Balham, London. (Photo: T. Pharoah)

49: Footway extensions provide space for other purposes, such as this cycleway exemption at a road closure. Cologne, Germany. (Photo: T. Pharoah)

APPLICATION

Footway extensions can be built wherever there is surplus carriageway space, and at all junctions, pedestrian crossing places and bus stops where on-street parking would otherwise be possible. An exception may be at junctions where an additional turning lane has to be maintained (e.g. in "mixed" or "traffic priority" streets).

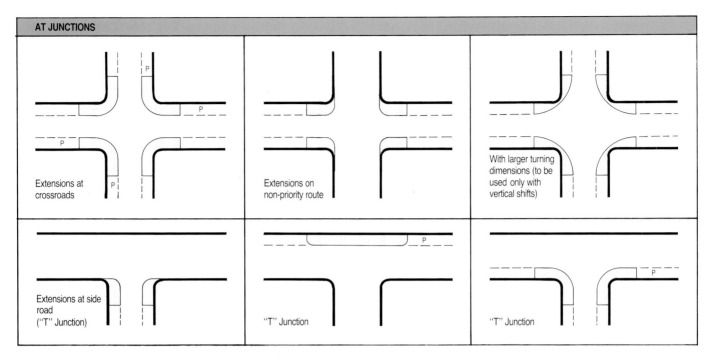

AT JUNCTIONS

Extensions at crossroads

Extensions on non-priority route

With larger turning dimensions (to be used only with vertical shifts)

Extensions at side road ("T" Junction)

"T" Junction

"T" Junction

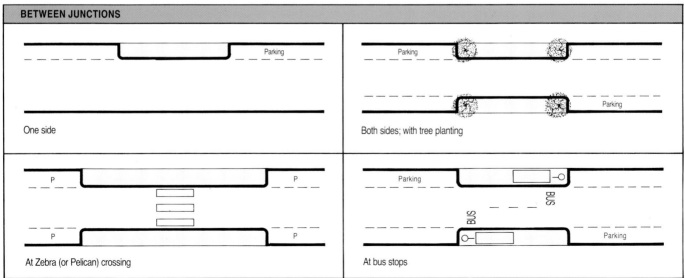

BETWEEN JUNCTIONS

One side

Both sides; with tree planting

At Zebra (or Pelican) crossing

At bus stops

DIAGRAM 3.22.1 FOOTWAY EXTENSIONS

DIMENSIONS

Extensions to footway areas may be as large as the provision of minimum appropriate carriageway width allows. On-street space for parking and loading also limits the extension. Extensions which define parking space should be a minimum of 1.8m from the original kerb line, with 2.25m being preferred.

SUPPORTING MEASURES

Planted areas help to define walking and staying areas, and in particular can direct pedestrians to the safest crossing place. Bollards can help to prevent vehicles overrunning corners, and provide additional security for pedestrians. The design of on-street parking should be integrated with footway extensions.

POSITIVE FACTORS

- Widely applicable and relatively inexpensive measure contributing to both safety and environmental objectives
- Can assist in economic and social enhancement of an area, for example if frontage activities such as shops, pubs and restaurants are provided with more outdoor space
- Can shelter and define permitted parking areas

NEGATIVE FACTORS

- None

50

50: Footway extensions are particularly valuable at pedestrian crossings: they improve visibility and shorten the distance which pedestrians have to cross. Souillac, France.
(Photo: T. Pharoah)

51: Trees planted within or near the carriageway need good support and protection. Here four stakes support the tree and iron rails prevent damage by vehicles. A water channel giving direct water access to the root system makes watering quicker and improves growth (note concrete gulley giving access to water channel). Aachen, Germany.
(Photo: T. Pharoah)

52: Kerbing is needed to prevent oil-polluted water from entering the plant bed, but extra protection should be provided where damage from vehicles is possible. Herne, Germany.
(Photo: T. Pharoah)

OBJECTIVES

- To limit forward views (see 3.8)
- To reduce physical and optical width (see 3.9 and 3.15)
- To define street spaces and activities
- To improve street appearance and the environment, including micro climate, noise and dust absorption

DESIGN FEATURES

Planting may be within footway and other pedestrian areas (low kerbs or grilles may be required), or within former carriageway areas (high kerbs or other means to prevent vehicle overrun required). Planted areas within the carriageway may stand clear of the kerb to allow existing surface drainage to be retained. Carriageway surface water should not drain into planted areas and such areas have to be checked for the location of underground pipes and cables. Newly planted trees should be semi-mature and supported with three or

51

52

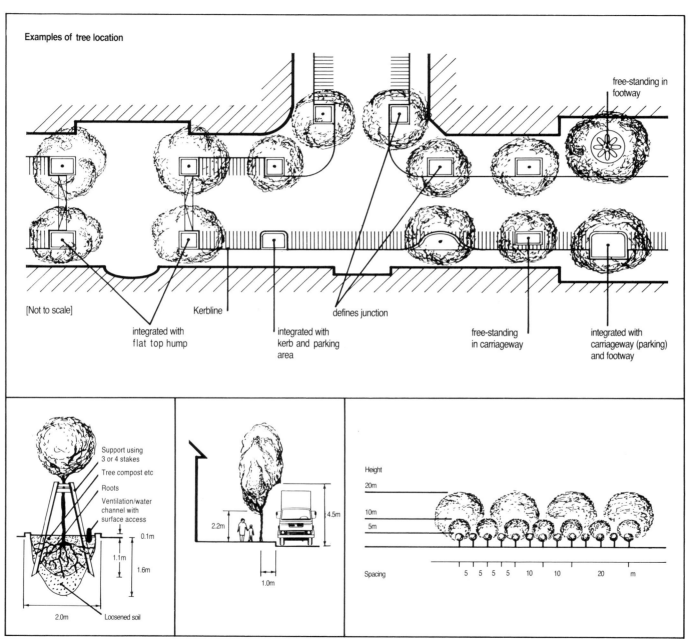

Examples of tree location

free-standing in footway

[Not to scale]

Kerbline

defines junction

integrated with
flat top hump

integrated with
kerb and parking
area

free-standing
in carriageway

integrated with
carriageway (parking)
and footway

Support using
3 or 4 stakes

Tree compost etc

Roots

Ventilation/water
channel with
surface access

0.1m

1.1m

1.6m

2.0m

Loosened soil

2.2m

4.5m

1.0m

Height

20m

10m

5m

Spacing

5   5   5   5   10   10   20   m

DIAGRAM 3.23.1 TREES IN THE STREET

53: Plant bed created within area of former carriageway. The bed in the foreground has been adopted by the frontage property owner, and is now adorned with a fine display of flowers.
(Photo: T. Pharoah)

54: Movable planters can be a useful temporary solution, as in this street outside a site due for redevelopment. Aachen, Germany.
(Photo: T. Pharoah)

53

54

depth is limited or where visibility must not be impaired. Planter boxes have the advantage that they can be easily moved and are particularly useful for temporary and experimental schemes.

Where planting is provided as part of a new development, the developer should be made responsible for the maintenance of the planted areas for a number of years until they are established. In the case of existing sites, the contract for planting may need to include maintenance for a given period of time. In any case liaison will be required with the District Council.

APPLICATION

Planting, and especially tree planting, is an essential ingredient of most traffic calming and environmental enhancement schemes. It may be limited by considerations of townscape character in some circumstances, and sometimes by soil and climate (e.g. in exposed coastal areas), but otherwise it is universally applicable. The advice of a landscape specialist should be sought to ensure that suitable species are specified.

DIMENSIONS

Shrubs and planters should not exceed 0.75m in height where they are likely to obscure the view of drivers or pedestrians. Trees should if possible be located in a planting area of at least 2 sq m. If planted adjacent to the carriageway, the trunk when fully grown should be at least 0.5m from the kerb. Varieties with a clean stem of about 1.5m do not obstruct drivers' vision. The

four substantial poles. These support structures not only protect the tree from wind and vandalism, but also contribute to the desired optical effect until the tree has matured. The type of tree, the reduced optical effect when trees are without leaves and the implications of leaf fall should all be taken into account.

Tree planting can be complemented by low shrubs or ground cover plants within the same area. This reduces weed growth and also contributes to the optical effect. Some areas may be suitable only for shrubs and ground cover plants, for example where the location and variety of tree have to be chosen to ensure adequate clearance above the carriageway.

SUPPORTING MEASURES

Kerbs need to be used to prevent surface water from the carriageway entering planted areas. Substantial hoops, rails or posts may be necessary to prevent damage by vehicles. Grilles can be used in footway areas as an alternative to kerbed areas. Tree supports have to be provided.

POSITIVE FACTORS

- Planting makes a major contribution to the required change of street character in traffic calming schemes, whilst at the same time improving the street scene and micro climate
- Trees provide vertical features at relatively low cost
- Frontagers may be encouraged to contribute to the creation and/or the maintenance of planted areas
- Planting can engender pride in the traffic calming scheme and in the street generally

NEGATIVE FACTORS

- May increase maintenance costs unless sponsored or adopted by frontagers or other bodies

55: Planters, mature trees and hanging baskets greatly improve the environment in Exeter High Street. (Photo: Devon County Council)

55

56: An integrated design of street furniture and paving can produce pleasing results. Cologne, Germany. (Photo: T. Pharoah)

57: Bollards can be removable to provide access, and can serve as meter posts. Cologne, Germany. (Photo: T. Pharoah)

3.24 STREET FURNITURE AND LIGHTING

OBJECTIVES

- To improve the functional and aesthetic qualities of the street
- To encourage the use of public space
- To enhance the safety and security of pedestrians
- To provide vertical elements adjacent to the carriageway (see 3.15)

DESIGN FEATURES

Bollards are used as an alternative or reinforcement to kerbs as a means of separating vehicle and pedestrian areas. To keep motor vehicles out, bollards have to be spaced about 1.5m apart. Lockable bollards can be provided where access exemptions are required. Bollards can serve other purposes, such as a resting post for the elderly or frail, cycle parking, parking meter pole, power supply point for market stalls. Bollards can be attractively designed, and can sometimes help to improve the street scene. However, long lengths should be broken up with other items such as planters, light columns and seats in appropriate cases.

Functional elements including seats, litter bins, telephone kiosks, cycle racks, bus shelters, and information points can be designed and grouped to create attractive focal points within the street. The creation of such areas should be considered at all places where pedestrian traffic is generated or

56

57

58: The siting of street furniture is important. In this example the telephone box, letter box, cycle rack, seat and tree are grouped together to good and practical effect. The Hague, Netherlands. (Photo: T. Pharoah)

converges, including entrances to parks, public buildings and pedestrian crossings. In particular, seating should be provided at regular intervals.

The location and design of street furniture needs to take account of the requirements of people with a visual handicap.

In "living" and "mixed priority" areas, standard traffic furniture and road markings are generally inappropriate. Warning signs are mostly unnecessary in areas with a speed limit of 20 mph or less. Lighting requirements are also less stringent in low speed areas, allowing for more imaginative and attractive designs.

APPLICATION

Lighting and street furniture should be designed and located consciously to enhance the "living" character of streets in built-up areas, and thus to reinforce the effectiveness of traffic calming measures.

DIMENSIONS

The inclusion of street furniture, its location and design needs to be planned with other elements in the traffic calming scheme. Some important dimensions to help in this planning work are given in Diagram 3.24.1.

SUPPORTING MEASURES

Not applicable.

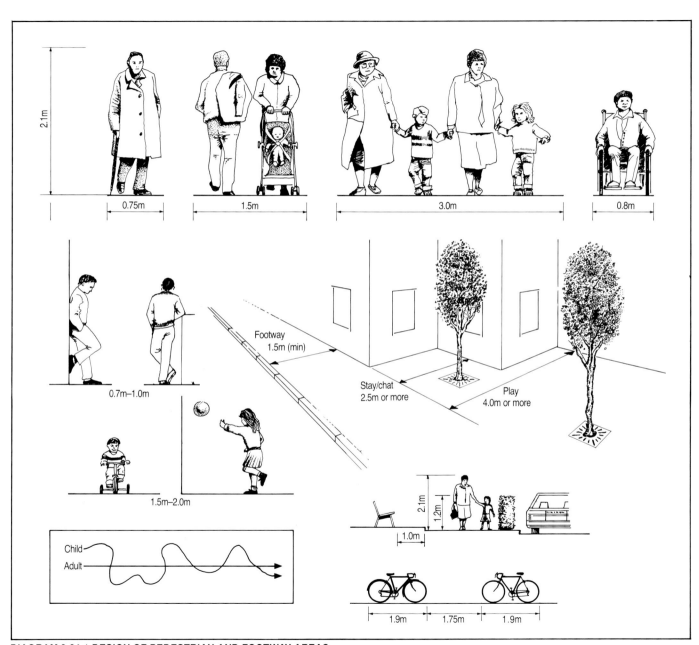

DIAGRAM 3.24.1 DESIGN OF PEDESTRIAN AND FOOTWAY AREAS

59: Slow speed areas allow lighting solutions that are in keeping with the street.
Bain-de-Bretagne, France.
(Photo: T. Pharoah)

60: Here a single lighting feature is used also as a signpost, a bus stop and a seating area, and thus provides a focal point in the centre of Eyam village, Derbyshire.
(Photo: T. Pharoah)

POSITIVE FACTORS
- Helps to enhance the functional and aesthetic qualities of the street, and thus to reinforce its "living" character

NEGATIVE FACTORS
- None if properly designed and sited

3.25 REGULATIONS

OBJECTIVES
- To legally reinforce the road user behaviour objectives of traffic calming designs

DESIGN FEATURES

The aim of all traffic calming schemes should be to achieve the desired effect through physical design rather than by regulations. Signs and markings should be kept to the minimum required. In the case of parking, the use of controlled zones with exceptions for designated bays may be appropriate. Where yellow lines are unavoidable it may be possible to use yellow bricks set in the road. Where possible, signs which are required should be integrated with buildings and street furniture to reduce their visual intrusiveness.

APPLICATION

Traffic calming measures do not generally involve amendments to traffic regulations other than the creation of zones with a speed limit of less than 30 mph. Some schemes will involve additional parking and waiting restrictions.

DIMENSIONS

Consideration should be given to the maximum size of area within which slow speeds apply. No part of a 20 mph zone should be further than 1 km from a road with a 30 mph or greater speed limit. Some restriction on the length of "mixed priority" through-road which is to be subject to the 20 mph speed limit may also be desirable.

SUPPORTING MEASURES

Legal changes need to be explained in the context of the objectives of traffic calming schemes through the usual media channels including educational projects, publicity material, public meetings and advertisements.

POSITIVE FACTORS
- Reinforces physical design and clarifies legal liability for road users

NEGATIVE FACTORS
- Involves the use of unsightly markings and/or signs

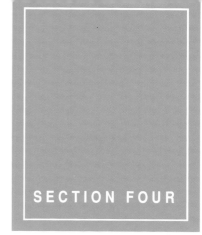

SCHEME EXAMPLES

This section, which outlines and illustrates various traffic calming schemes implemented both in this country and on the continent, is intended to stimulate thought. Certain details of the "as built" schemes may differ from those shown in some cases.

All the schemes are described under the following sub-headings:
Context
Objectives
Description
Cost
Assessment

For consistency all speeds are quoted in miles per hour. For the continental schemes 20 mph, 25 mph and 30 mph correspond to 30 kph, 40 kph and 50 kph respectively.

LIST OF SCHEMES

RESIDENTIAL AREAS:
Aachen, Forst (Germany)
Berlin, Moabit
    Area-wide Project (Germany)
Buxtehude, Area-wide Project (Germany)
Cologne, Nippes District (Germany)
Cologne, Wittekind Strasse (Germany)
Exeter, Burnthouse Lane
Exeter, Newtown
Haringey, Mount Pleasant Road
Leicester, Worthington Street
Plymouth, Victoria Road, St. Budeaux
Sheffield, Tinsley
Yealmpton, Yealm Park

CITY CENTRES:

Exeter, High Street/Queen Street
Exeter, Bedford Street
Frankfurt City Centre (Germany)
Sheffield, High Street
Torquay, Fleet Street

URBAN MAIN ROADS:

Cologne, Kalker Strasse (Germany)
Eindhoven, Leenderweg (Netherlands)
Wandsworth, St. John's Hill

SMALL TOWNS AND
SUBURBAN MAIN ROADS:

Barnstaple, Boutport Street
Barnstaple, High Street
Barnstaple, Tuly Street
Borehamwood, Shenley Road
Brixham, Fore Street
Buntingford, High Street
Dartmouth, Town Centre
Hennef, Frankfurter Strasse (Germany)
Langenfeld, Hauptstrasse (Germany)
Sidmouth, Town Centre
Totnes, The Plains

VILLAGE THROUGH ROADS:

Dulmen Buldern Village (Germany)
Much, Village Centre (Germany)

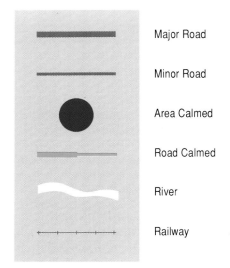

KEY TO LOCATION PLANS

Major Road

Minor Road

Area Calmed

Road Calmed

River

Railway

─────	Building Line
─┴─┴─┴─	Property Divisions
─────	Property Boundary
─────	Kerb Line with Upstand
─ ─ ─ ─	Kerb Line with No or Low Upstand
··········	No Change of Level
▨	Road Markings
▨	Public Footway
▨	Carriageway
▨	Shared Space (Footway and Carriageway)
▨	Cycleway
▨	Parking
▨	Occasional Strip
▨	Textured Area

▭	Cushion
⊠	Plateau
•→	Traffic Signals
⊠	Ramp, at Flat Top Hump
▲	Vehicle Crossover Point
▽△	Round Top Hump
⊢• ⊢•⊣	Lighting
▯ ▥	Seating
B	Bus Stop
• • • •	Bollards
◯	Tree
▢	Planter
▨	Grassed Area
→ → →	Direction of Vehicle Travel
─⌐_⌐─	Partial Street Plan

CONTEXT

Forst is a suburb of Aachen about 2 km east of the city centre with a loose structure of mixed residential, commercial and industrial activity. The area adopted for an area-wide traffic calming scheme totals about 0.5 km^2 and is cut across by a major radial road (Trierer Strasse). Public consultation took place in 1987 and by 1990 20 mph zones had been designated, with physical measures in several streets completed. No work had yet been undertaken on Trierer Strasse, however.

OBJECTIVES

The aims were: to improve safety, especially for non-motorised traffic; to reduce through traffic (formerly up to 500 vehicles per hour); to achieve speeds more compatible with a living environment (85 percentile speeds of 30 mph were considered

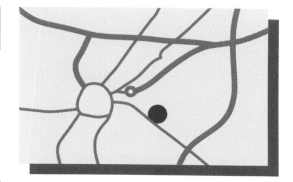

too fast);to rationalise on-street parking; and to increase planting.

DESCRIPTION

The entire residential area became a 20 mph zone, with entrances to the zone emphasized by use of narrowed carriageways, trees and the standard zone sign. Within the zone, speeds are limited by a mixture of measures including

1: Entrance to the Forst 20 mph zone at a traffic signal intersection. Vehicles entering the zone are slowed by a narrowing which incorporates the standard zone sign, and trees to provide a gateway effect.
(Photo: T. Pharoah)

2: A crossroads plateau provides convenient crossing for pedestrians while slowing traffic speeds. Definition and visual interest are provided by trees planted within the carriageway.
(Photo: T. Pharoah)

1

2

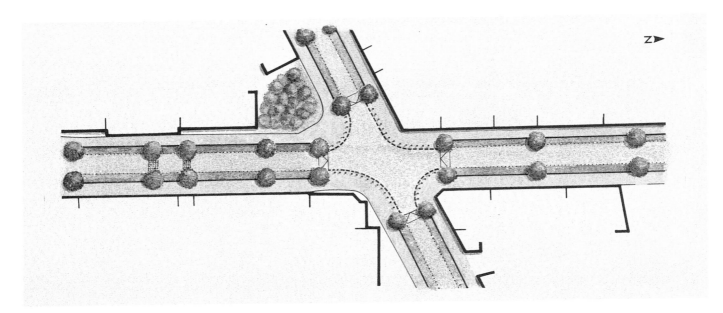

3: Planted areas help to define the footway at a "T" junction, and create sheltered parking bays. Note the integration of the planted area with the existing kerb.
(Photo: T. Pharoah)

carriageway constrictions, plateaux and reductions in the "optical width" using semi-mature trees at intervals of not more than 20m. Trees are planted within the carriageway, thus serving to define parking areas. Selected areas are converted to "mixed precincts" (or shared spaces). Cycleways will be provided on the main streets but are not necessary within the 20 mph zone. Residential courtyards currently used for parking will be landscaped and converted for play and other living activities.

COST

Not known.

ASSESSMENT

Not available: scheme not complete.

3

4

4: Tree planting adds to the appearance of this street, and defines the on-street parking bays. (Photo: T. Pharoah)

5: The footways also are not forgotten. Here red bricks lead from the apartment block entrances to new planted areas. People leaving the apartments thus see trees and shrubs rather than parked cars. (Photo: T. Pharoah)

5

6: A constriction simply achieved by planting trees and shrubs within the carriageway. Bollards help to protect these areas from vehicles. The planted areas are free-standing so that surface drainage is not affected.
(Photo: T. Pharoah)

7: Close up of the Moabit cushion, which allows cyclists to pass in comfort. This one is built within an existing asphalt surface.
(Photo: T. Pharoah)

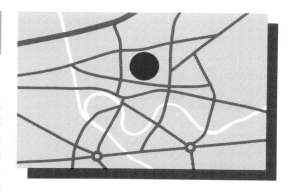

CONTEXT

Moabit is an inner-city district of Berlin with 7,000 people employed and a resident population of 30,000 people living mainly in traditional style apartment blocks of 5 or 6 storeys, built around the turn of the century. Most of the streets are laid out on a grid pattern, and are fairly broad. In 1980 Moabit was chosen as one of the six Federal demonstrations of area-wide traffic calming, and the scheme was implemented in the mid 1980s. The area covered was roughly $1km^2$. The main traffic roads were to have been included in the scheme, but the proposals ran into political opposition from Berlin city/state authority. This example therefore concerns only the local residential streets.

OBJECTIVES

The scheme aimed: to improve traffic safety; to make walking and cycling easier; to create more possibilities for neighbourhood recreation and development; and to improve the local environment.

DESCRIPTION

The "slow speed" approach was adopted using the German standard sign (now adopted by several countries). This sign indicates a maximum speed equivalent to walking or running pace, equal priority for

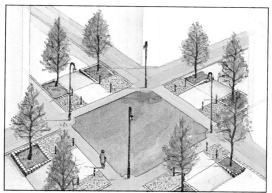

PLATEAU

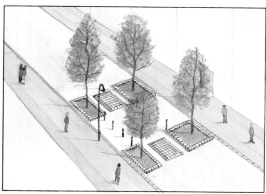

CUSHION

all road users including pedestrians, and that children are allowed to play in the street. Former one-way streets in the area were abolished. This change of rules reinforced physical measures that were introduced to slow motor traffic and to provide more space for pedestrians and for recreation and planting.

The main speed reduction measures are cushions, plateaux and selective carriageway narrowing. These measures are spaced about 40m - 60m apart, and in places cushions are located in pairs, which creates a better speed reduction effect. Carriageway constrictions are achieved with planted areas and coincide with cushions or ramps. One particularly wide street has been converted to a linear park, with only a narrow carriageway remaining at one side. Footways are continued across junctions with plateaux. Planting, which together with other environmental treatment now occupies more than 6,000m^2 of former carriageway space, is a major element of the scheme and the number of trees in the area has been doubled.

BEFORE

AFTER

BREMER STRASSE

AVERAGE SPEED PROFILE OF TYPICAL STREET IN MOABIT

6

7

8

9

8: The street that became a park. Most of the carriageway in Waldstrasse now provides space for rest and play and is adorned with numerous trees and shrubs. Much of the original asphalt surface is retained, partly for economy but partly for children to use for roller-boots, etc.
(Photo: P. Bowers)

9: Traditional granite setts have been re-used to create interesting textures, and to help with speed reduction. Smooth paving is provided for pedestrians to cross, however. Bollards keep vehicles out of this rest area.
(Photo: T. Pharoah)

Major efforts were made to involve the public at every stage of the scheme. A special team was established and three main stages of participation were carried out. Information stands, public meetings and questionnaires were all used. In one street a full-scale mock-up of the proposed measures was used to obtain public opinion on specific features.

COST

The cost was about £1.8 million for the whole scheme, or about £10 per m^2 of street space. The cost was kept much lower than earlier traffic calming schemes by retaining kerbs and drainage, and by reusing existing materials such as granite setts.

ASSESSMENT

The scheme has had a positive effect on road safety. The number of personal injury accidents has been reduced by 41%, deaths have been cut by 57%, serious injuries by 36% and slight injuries by 34%. Accident reductions have been more significant for pedestrians and cyclists than for car users. Child injuries have been cut by 69%. These changes can be set against a decrease in motor traffic but an increase in pedestrian and cycle traffic in the area. It has been calculated that savings in accident costs in the first two years alone exceeded the entire capital cost of the scheme.

Average traffic speed has almost halved to 12 mph, and the 85 percentile value dropped from 31 mph to around 15 mph.

10: Speed reduction is achieved with the famous Berlin cushion, sometimes placed in twos or threes, as shown here. The optical width of the street is reduced with narrowings and intensive tree planting, which also helps to mask parked vehicles. (Photo: T. Pharoah)

10

Hardly any vehicle travels faster than 20 mph. In addition, a calm style of driving is adopted by most drivers, with less braking and acceleration, and fewer sudden turning movements.

Traffic noise has been reduced by 5 dBA or more in most streets, and vehicle emissions have also been reduced. This is due partly to the slower and calmer driving and partly to reductions in traffic volume of up to 40%.

The scheme is popular with residents and traders, with the greater safety and particularly the increased greenery being appreciated. Some residents have taken on sponsorship of planted areas. Cafe owners now rent street areas for outdoor tables.

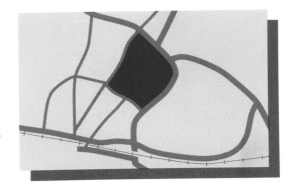

BUXTEHUDE · AREA-WIDE PROJECT · GERMANY

CONTEXT

Buxtehude is a medium-sized town (population about 30,000) lying 35 km west of Hamburg, Germany. The northern half of the town, with a population of 11,000 and including an historic town centre, was chosen as one of the six Federal demonstration projects for area-wide traffic calming. The scheme has been widely acclaimed as achieving all-round benefits at reasonable cost.

OBJECTIVES

The aim was to relieve some of the problems typical of a medium-sized town, namely: intrusion from a high density of through traffic; danger resulting from high traffic speeds in residential areas; and a physical and commercial environment in need of upgrading. The aim was also to promote pedestrian and cycle traffic and public transport.

DESCRIPTION

The approach was to avoid the barrier effect of traffic streets running through the area by introducing measures to restrain or discourage traffic.

The area-wide scheme was implemented in two stages. The first stage

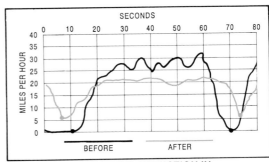

REPRESENTATIVE SPEED REDUCTION IN ALTLANDER STRASSE

11

12

13

12: Speeds are kept to 20 mph on this distributor road with a series of narrowings and flat top humps located where pedestrians need to cross. Speed reducing features are readily identified with the distinctive red and white paving. Planting and new lighting improves the overall appearance of the street.
(Photo: T. Pharoah)

13: This residential street has been closed to motor traffic except for access, and converted to a two-way bicycle road linking with the town centre. The effective width has been halved using planted areas on one side.
(Photo: T. Pharoah)

footpath and cycle crossings at important junctions, carriageway narrowing, redesigned on-street parking, and the creation of more and better facilities for pedestrians and cyclists. A planned third stage to exclude through traffic by road closures and barriers turned out to be unnecessary.

COST

The total investment up to completion in 1987 was about £1.7 million, or roughly £70 per head of population living in the area, spread over four or five years. The final cost per m^2 of road space (including footways) was about £4.60 at 1986 prices. One street (Altlander Strasse) was in need of reconstruction anyway, and this was carried out at a cost of about £40,000.

ASSESSMENT

Speeds have been reduced to an 85 percentile value of slightly more than 20 mph, but the measures enable a calm style of driving in third gear with low engine revolutions. This is considered to be within

was implemented at low cost and included a change of speed limit from 30 mph to 20 mph (apart from a central pedestrian zone and two "slow speed" areas), a change of priority rule at junctions whereby drivers must give way to traffic entering from the right, and some narrowing of carriageways using plant tubs and other temporary objects.

Stage two involved more permanent physical measures to create a self-enforcing speed limit of 20 mph, and to improve both the functional and aesthetic elements of the streets involved. This included the provision of new surfaces and lighting at all entrances,

BUXTEHUDE MODEL PROJECT - KEY TO PLAN

MEASURES	NARROWING		
pedestrian zone	one side	ramp	
30 kph zone	both sides	additional ramp/narrowing	
50 kph streets	one side with ramp	lorries prohibited	
(Bahnhof Str. now 30 kph)	both sides with ramp	cycle street (cars for access only)	
		Research measurement location	

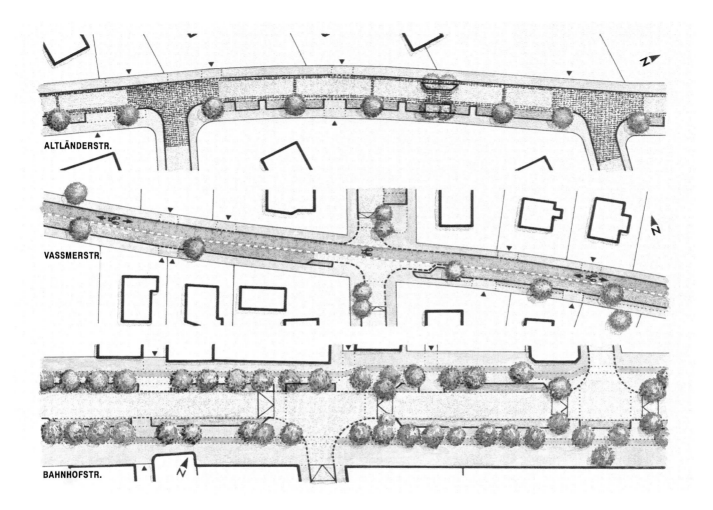

ALTLÄNDERSTR.

VASSMERSTR.

BAHNHOFSTR.

the spirit of traffic calming, and has produced considerable environmental as well as safety benefits.

Within the 20 mph zone, accident severity has reduced considerably, though the number of light damage accidents has increased. Cyclist accidents also increased compared to non-treated areas, though it is not known whether this is due to increased cycling activity. Since the number of accidents is fairly low, the results can only be indicative of changes in safety.

Noise from passing vehicles has decreased by 4-5 dBA (equivalent to a halving of traffic volume) due to slower and calmer driving. Vehicle emissions have also

14: The footway and cycleway in Bahnhof Strasse are separated from the main carriageway by parking bays and a green verge with newly planted trees, which helps to reduce the dominating effect of heavy traffic.
(Photo: T. Pharoah)

15: Tree planting helps to create a boulevard atmosphere in busy Bahnhof Strasse, which also has a 20 mph speed limit. Shallow humps are provided at intervals, one of which is seen here being negotiated by a bus.
(Photo: T. Pharoah)

16: Footways and cycleways are kept at a continuous level across side roads and access ways, with ramped approaches to slow turning vehicles. The absence of any change of level is particularly comfortable for pedestrians with buggies etc., as shown here.
(Photo: T. Pharoah)

14

15

16

been reduced as detailed below, though petrol consumption has increased by 7%.

Carbon Monoxide . . 20%
Hydro Carbons 10%
Nitrogen Oxide 33%

Questionnaire surveys revealed a marked change in attitudes to traffic speed after completion of the scheme. Drivers and residents were asked to say what speed they considered appropriate for residential areas and the results from the before and after surveys are as shown.

The traffic calming investment is also associated with an increase in Buxtehude's commercial vitality. Previous trends of decline have been reversed with more people shopping in Buxtehude and fewer people driving into Hamburg for this purpose. Environmental enhancement has also attracted more tourists to the town.

Appropriate speed in residential areas	Drivers		Residents	
	Before	After	Before	After
20 mph	27%	67%	39%	76%
30 mph	46%	6%	49%	7%

CONTEXT

The high density housing of Cologne's Nippes District consists of mainly 3-5 storey apartments. The area is situated outside Cologne's second ring-road about 2 km north of the Cathedral, and is bisected by a main radial road, Neusser Strasse. Following local consultations, the City Council implemented traffic calming in the streets west of Neusser Strasse during the mid-1980s. Action had earlier been taken to limit through traffic by the partial closure of Mauenheimer Strasse at its junction with Neusser Strasse, and by one-way streets.

OBJECTIVES

The aims were: to further discourage through traffic while making access for local traffic easier; to slow traffic to 20 mph or less; to provide safety for children playing in the street and walking to school; and to create more attractive and useful public spaces particularly by planting and reducing asphalt areas.

DESCRIPTION

The first phase was the creation of a slow-speed area (under about 15 mph) with streets reconstructed to provide two footways, defined parking bays and a shared-space for all traffic including pedestrians and cyclists. Surplus former carriageway space was converted to either footway, parking, planting or open space,

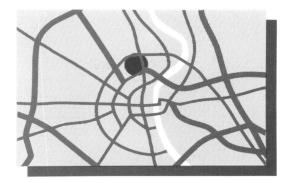

17: Through traffic has gone from Baudiplatz, and the local traffic travels slowly through the reconstructed area. Low kerbs help people with a visual handicap to locate the vehicle areas, while bollards keep drivers in their place. Planted areas are protected with iron rails. (Photo: T. Pharoah)

especially at Schillplatz, where a new square was created in front of the church. Over 30 new trees were planted in the street to define the parking bays and speed reduction measures. Slow driving is ensured by enforced turns and changes of level (see photo 17). Speed reducing measures occur every 50m. Although pedestrians may walk anywhere, they also have exclusive footway areas separated from the areas where

17

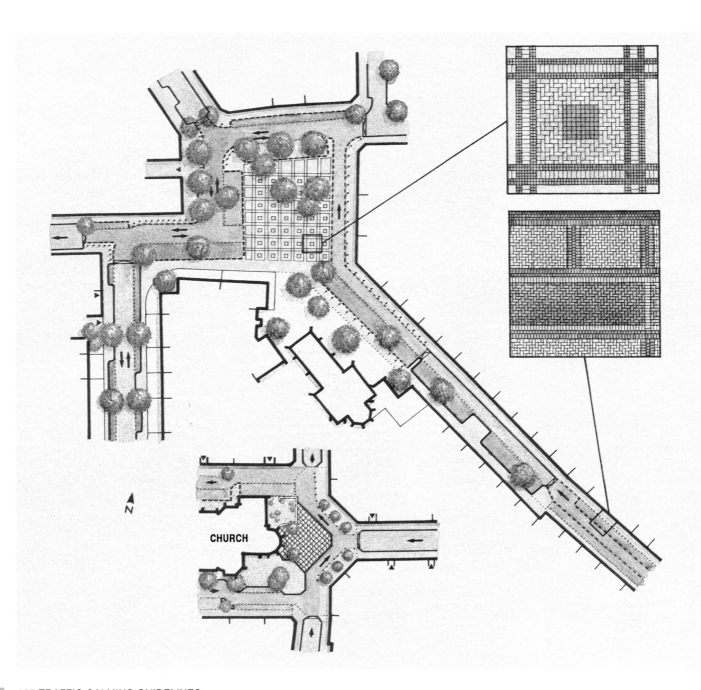

CHURCH

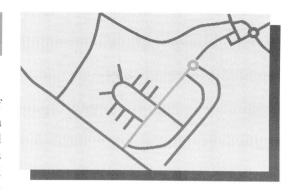

CONTEXT

Burnthouse Lane is the main artery of an extensive residential area. It is a distributor road and connects a major radial road to a large district of Exeter known as Heavitree. Two schools are sited on this road which also acts as a main access route to a Secondary School and a Nursery School. There are shops, churches, a surgery, a village hall, and a public house along its length. It was a long straight road with uninterrupted visibility of 0.5 km. This combined with a width of 12.5m, gave rise to considerable volumes of traffic on what is essentially a residential road, with motorists

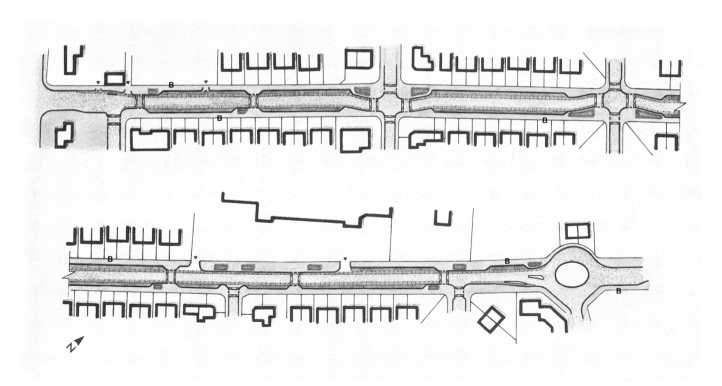

23

24

23: Flat top humps, lateral shifts and footway extensions at approach to junction. Planting, including raised red brick flower beds, adds to the street scene. (Photo: Devon County Council)

24: The narrowed street with cycle tracks and sheltered parking. The dedicated cycle lane at the junction leads to the Exe Cycle Route. (Photo: Devon County Council)

travelling at high and illegal speeds. There were a significant number of accidents with a high proportion involving pedestrians or cyclists.

OBJECTIVES

Burnthouse Lane performs several functions, some of which conflict and it was, therefore, decided to set three primary objectives: reduce traffic speed; reduce accidents; and improve the environment. The local community was involved in the development of the scheme.

DESCRIPTION

The main carriageway width was reduced from 12.5m to 5.5m wide, with an additional 1m wide cycle track on both sides and sheltered parking was provided. Flat top humps were installed along the route and at the junctions, including the side roads

entering Burnthouse Lane. Lateral shifts were introduced at the approaches to the junctions.

The road and sheltered parking was surfaced in bitumen macadam, the cycle track was surfaced with red slurry seal and small (300mm x 450mm) grey concrete slabs were used for the footway. The road humps were formed by fixing brindle coloured concrete blocks to the carriageway on an epoxy mortar bed with bitumen macadam approach ramps. Accesses across the footway to private drives were formed in grey concrete blocks.

Raised planters were constructed in red brick and this, combined with the planting of trees and the change in alignment, succeeded in removing the impression of a wide straight fast road.

Lighting columns with long outreach arms were provided at the back of the footway. In addition, a lighting column with a spherical lantern was provided on the footway at each side of the road humps, which has the double benefit of enhancing the lighting at these sites where pedestrians

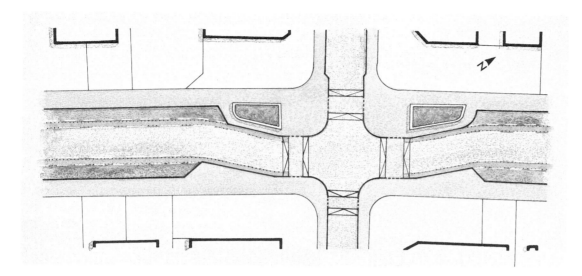

are most likely to cross and also acting as a means of drawing the motorist's attention to the road humps themselves.

Additional footway and planters were provided outside Bradley Rowe school which has provided a pleasant area where parents may gather while waiting for their children.

COST

The cost was £220,000 for the total length of scheme of 0.6 km.

ASSESSMENT

The Burnthouse Lane Traffic Calming Scheme has been a success in terms of the original objectives set. Before the scheme was carried out some 37% of vehicles exceeded 30 mph. The 85 percentile speed was 34 mph, with maximum speeds being recorded between 50 and 55 mph. Following the completion of the scheme, the 85 percentile speed had fallen to 24 mph with maximum speeds of between 29 and 33 mph being recorded. At the road humps themselves the speeds are approximately 14 mph. The annual rate of accidents is lower than before the scheme was implemented particularly in the under 11 years age group and the severity of accidents has been reduced. A 12% reduction in traffic flows during peak hours has been achieved.

The use of quality materials and planting has contributed to the environmental improvements and resulted in the residents of Burnthouse Lane taking a renewed pride in this road. On the negative side, there have been some complaints about traffic transferring to alternative adjacent routes.

25: Widened footways and restricted vehicle access achieved significant improvements in this early scheme.
(Photo: Devon County Council)

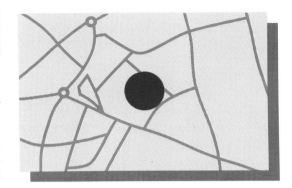

CONTEXT

Newtown is an old residential district of Exeter, flanked by a major radial road to the south and by the Inner Bypass. The main roads serving the area are almost parallel and closely spaced. On-street parking was prevalent and the general environment of the area needed upgrading.

OBJECTIVES

The original aim of the scheme was to enhance the environment of the area under the then current General Improvement Area Schemes initiative. The scheme eventually implemented in 1973 had rather wider objectives of resolving conflict at the closely spaced junctions at the ends of residential roads and reducing the amount of through traffic.

DESCRIPTION

The following measures were taken:
- Stopping up sections of residential roads and creating additional footway areas
- Provision of off-street parking for residents

COST

Not known.

ASSESSMENT

The stopping up of sections of roads and giving these areas over to pedestrians has helped solve some of the traffic problems and, by "calming traffic", contributed to the environmental improvement of the area.

25

CONTEXT

Mount Pleasant Road is a residential road in the east of the London Borough of Haringey, used as a "rat run" by drivers seeking to avoid congestion on the A10 trunk road and other main roads. A previous attempt to remove "rat running" traffic was stopped by the Department of Transport. Over the 1km length there were on average more than 4 accidents each year including accidents involving children.

OBJECTIVES

The objectives were to reduce traffic flows, vehicle speeds and accidents.

DESCRIPTION

The solution adopted was a series of 16 road humps (installed according to the Road Hump Regulations 1986) and 10 carriageway narrowings at road hump locations along the length of the road. Seven of the narrowings reduced carriageway width to 3.5 m and were signed on both approaches "Road Narrows on Both Sides". In addition, footway extensions were constructed in most side entrances to control vehicle parking and improve pedestrian visibility.

COST

The cost was approximately £70,000.

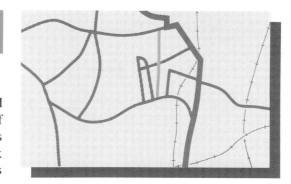

26: Road hump and carriageway narrowing at a zebra crossing. (Photo: London Borough of Haringey)

26

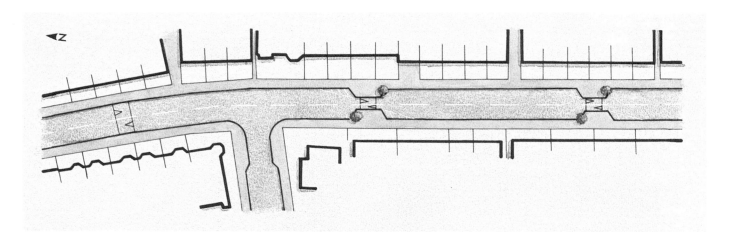

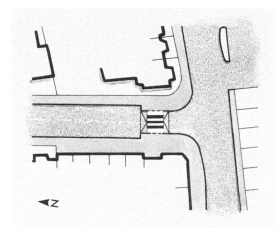

27: Carriageway narrowing at a road hump showing arrow boards, and bollards to discourage parking. (Photo: London Borough of Haringey)

27

ASSESSMENT

The scheme was introduced with the backing of local residents and implemented in early 1990. Before and after traffic flows are given below.

	AM peak (vph)	PM peak (vph)	24 hour (vph)
Before	935	875	11,221
After	754	651	7,756

Where the displaced traffic has gone is still the subject of study. Preliminary assessments, however, suggest that many vehicles have "evaporated".

Vehicle speeds have been reduced from a mean speed of 34 mph (85 percentile = 39 mph) to 26 mph (85 percentile = 28 mph). No accidents had been recorded in the first seven months after the scheme came into operation.

28: Shared surface showing street furniture and coloured pavers. (Photo: Leicester City Council)

CONTEXT

A combination of circumstances led Leicester City Council to create a "Woonerf" type scheme for Worthington Street in 1985/6. Worthington Street is lined with 80 terraced houses fronting directly onto the street. Of several streets in the area linking two heavily trafficked roads, Worthington Street was the only one remaining open to through traffic, with a peak flow of about 130 vehicles per hour. The availability of

Urban Programme funds allowed a comprehensive environmental traffic scheme to be implemented, and the City Council was keen to apply the principles

28

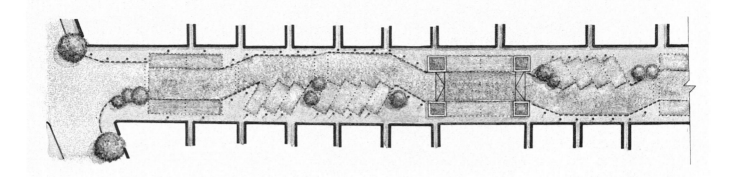

29: Lateral shift in the carriageway formed by angled parking bays defined with planting and cast iron bollards. (Photo: Leicester City Council)

established by the Dutch "Woonerf" schemes (see section on "shared surfaces").

OBJECTIVES

The aim was to transform Worthington Street into an area principally for the relaxation and enjoyment of its residents through the creation of an open space environment, but, without closing it to traffic. Two principal objectives were: to deter unnecessary through traffic and encourage vehicles using the street to travel slowly and carefully; and radically to improve the environment for the benefit of residents and pedestrians.

DESCRIPTION

The traditional carriageway and kerb-defined footways were replaced with a new surface, and a range of different colours were used to define, in particular, areas to which vehicles are restricted. Speed restraint was achieved with a narrow carriageway incorporating lateral shifts and a flat top hump. The ramps are provided at strategic locations and marked by brick planters decorated with fleurs-de-lys and rosette embossed brick courses. These complement decorative brickwork in adjacent buildings.

Clay pavers bordered with soldier courses of red brick form the road-way and the 39 parking bays are picked out in dark brown paving with cast iron bollards and railings. Alternate angled parking is

29

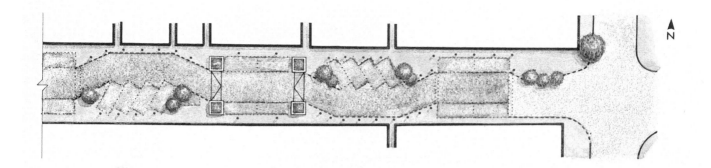

provided together with some lateral parking. Distinct buff-coloured pavers create forecourts contiguous to the houses.

Victorian style street lighting was installed, and trees and shrubs planted to soften the overall design. Hanging baskets and window boxes are mounted on house fronts where owners have agreed to maintain them.

Residents' participation in the scheme was both extensive and productive. They requested (and got) more parking spaces incorporated into the scheme, and they made the final choice between two alternative detailed designs. A street committee was taken on a tour of the City Council's other street improvement works to help them select appropriate street furniture. A survey of residents at that time revealed that two thirds were in favour of the scheme.

COST

The total cost including professional fees was about £180,000, met partly from Urban Programme grants.

ASSESSMENT

The introduction of more attractive paving and street furniture has produced a pleasant residential environment. Traffic speeds and volumes have been reduced, though some cars still travel too fast. Some maintenance problems have arisen from petty vandalism and litter. Although refuse

30: Speed reduction ramp between brick planters.
(Photo: Leicester City Council)

30

31

therefore had to be achieved through design measures under existing legislative provision. The main problems related to parking (allowed only in the defined bays, rather than restricted elsewhere) and the legal status of pedestrians once the defined footway had been removed.

Worthington Street now falls within a wider area (with about 4,500 households) identified for a demonstration scheme to improve facilities for pedestrians and the environment. This will be carried out as part of the "feet first" initiative promoted by the Local Authority Associations and Transport 2000.

31: Parking bays defined with dark brown pavers and cast iron bollards. Railings also add interest to the street scene outside a local shop.
(Photo: Leicester City Council)

and cleaning services have not experienced any problems, the lack of storage for "wheely bins" tends to spoil the street scene.

Integral to the scheme, underground services were renewed and this accounted for one sixth of the total cost. It is thus hoped to reduce the potential for unsympathetic remedial works by statutory undertakers.

No systematic evaluation of the scheme has been carried out, partly because the scheme was seen as being specific to the circumstances of Worthington Street and partly because grant funds are no longer available to allow replication of the solution elsewhere.

An attempt was made to introduce supporting legislation, akin to that which exists in the Netherlands for "Woonerf" schemes, in the Leicestershire Act of 1984, but without success. The inherent emphasis on pedestrian priority over vehicles

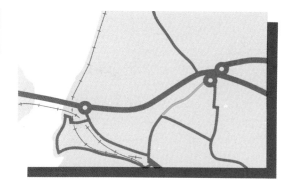

CONTEXT

Victoria Road is a long road varying in width from less than 7m to over 10m serving mainly as a major residential road in the St. Budeaux district of Plymouth. Suburban shopping and commercial activities occur along the middle section of this road. Following the opening of St. Budeaux Bypass in 1988, "after" studies indicated that traffic flow in Victoria Road had increased by over a third (from under 8,000 to over 11,000 vehicles per 12 hour day). This was mainly because trips starting and finishing in St. Budeaux were being diverted to Victoria Road when access to the Bypass from the adjacent roads was restricted or closed. Further road closure at Victoria Road would cause considerable inconvenience to St. Budeaux residents themselves and traffic orders would be difficult to enforce. Therefore it is proposed to introduce

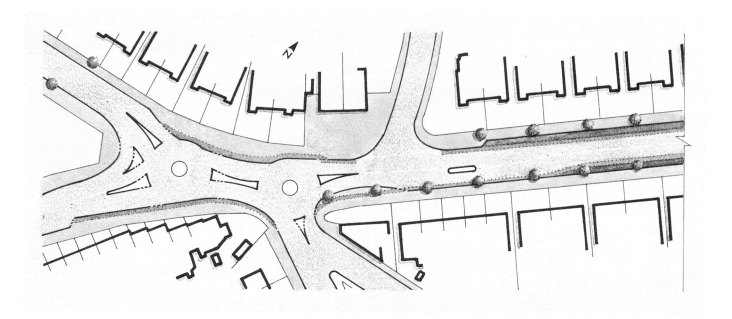

comprehensive traffic calming measures accompanied by environmental improvements.

OBJECTIVES

The concept proposed is to change the image of Victoria Road from that of a major traffic route and to deter extraneous traffic.

DESCRIPTION

Physical measures to slow motor traffic and to provide additional crossing points for pedestrians are proposed. These measures include the introduction of mini roundabouts, narrowing of the wide carriageway, provision of cycle tracks, removal of some yellow lines to allow parking, and highway enhancement such as repaving of footways and landscaping.

COST

The estimated cost is £250,000 to £300,000.

ASSESSMENT

Scheme not yet undertaken.

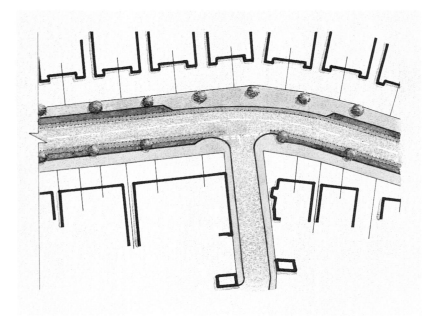

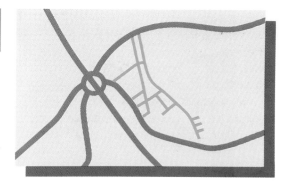

CONTEXT

Tinsley lies in the Don Valley, some 6 km to the north-east of Sheffield city centre. The traffic calming scheme at Tinsley is one of four selected by the Department of Transport in 1990 to spearhead the application of new 20 mph zone regulations.

The general area is industrial in character, but the 20 mph zone is residential with shops and recreational facilities. There are two distinct housing types having different socio-economic and racial mixes. One part is pre-1919 terraced housing with properties close to roads, no off-street parking and grid type road layout. This area has Housing Action Area (HAA) status, and limited finance for environmental street works was available. In contrast the other part of the area consists of post-war semi-detached housing with gardens and off-street parking.

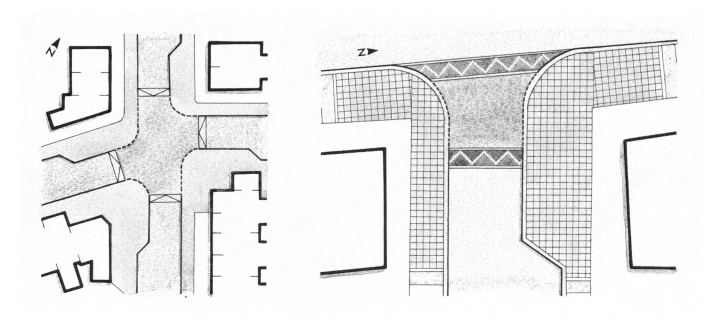

32: Junction treatment nearing completion in Stage 1 showing ramped plateau with chevron markings, extended footway, defined parking and tree "pocket". (Photo: K. Platt)

32

There are bus routes on roads which are also used as links between major roads. To reach the recreation ground and schools, children cross residential roads with high vehicle speeds and much on-street parking. Child pedestrian accidents tend to be concentrated along these roads.

OBJECTIVES

The scheme was designed, with the agreement of the people of Tinsley, to incorporate speed reduction measures within environmental improvement works associated with the HAA. Extensions to the initial zone will address the problem of child pedestrian accidents on the surrounding roads.

DESCRIPTION

Each entry point or "gateway" to the zone is treated by carriageway narrowing, a flat top hump, and zone entry signs. Plateaux have been constructed at junctions within the zone. Footways are extended thus creating crossing places with low kerb upstands, and short crossing distances.

Visibility is also improved if parking is confined to the lengths of sheltered parking defined by the footway extensions. Longer lengths of road have intermediate flat top humps.

The flat top humps are 100mm high and trials involving emergency services resulted in ramp gradients on the access type roads of 1 in 8. Ramp gradients will be less severe on the local distributor roads.

Materials used are brindle block-paved ramps incorporating white reflective blocks to produce chevron patterns. Flat top humps are surfaced in red bitumen macadam. Narrowings are surfaced in small element paving while block paving is used for forecourts. Trees have been planted where underground services permit and street lighting has been improved.

COST

Not available.

ASSESSMENT

The first stage of the scheme was implemented in 1990. Surveys of traffic speed and volume and of residents' opinions will be undertaken with the co-operation of the Transport and Road Research Laboratory (TRRL).

CONTEXT

Yealm Park is a residential development at the edge of Yealmpton. On-street parking occurred along most of the estate roads and vehicles tended to travel at speeds higher than appropriate for residential roads. The area also lacked soft landscaping.

OBJECTIVES

The objectives were to provide a better environment for the residents as well as to provide off-street parking, reduce vehicle speeds and improve safety.

DESCRIPTION

The approach was to introduce a one-way traffic system around the centre of the estate, construct flat top humps/pedestrian crossings together with carriageway constrictions around the estate road circuit and carry out a junction improvement. Additional car parking spaces were provided and drop crossings were introduced to facilitate off-street parking. A high quality planting scheme was implemented at existing and new verge areas.

COST

The cost was £30,400.

ASSESSMENT

The reduced carriageway width at the flat top humps has lowered driving speeds

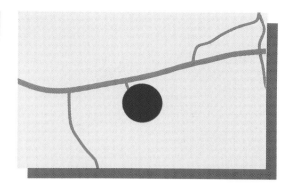

33: Junction layout with paved carriageway constriction at point of no entry.
(Photo: Devon County Council)

and made crossing the road easier for the residents. The problem of on-street parking has also been improved significantly in most of the estate roads. The introduction of trees, new verge areas and new and contrasting clay paver surfaces has resulted in a softer street scene and a pleasanter environment.

33

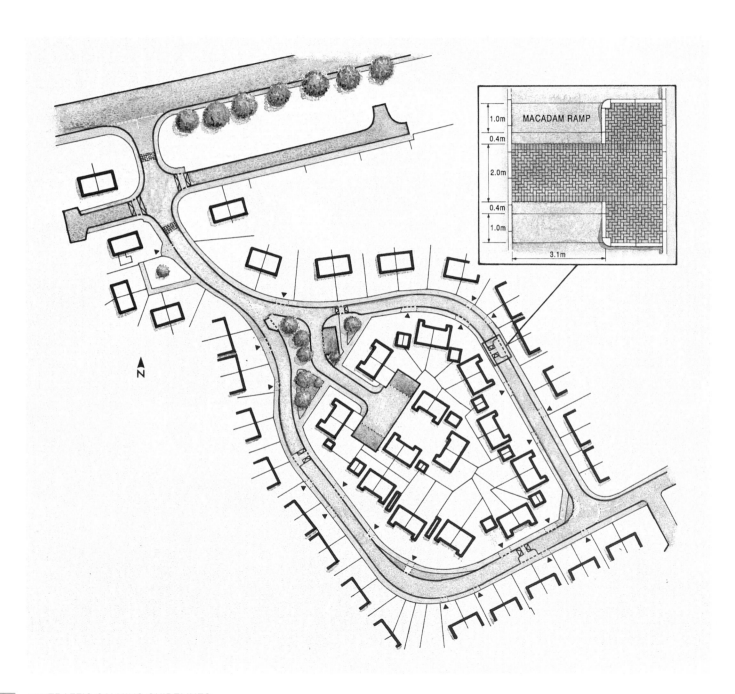

MACADAM RAMP

1.0m
0.4m
2.0m
0.4m
1.0m

3.1m

CONTEXT

Exeter is the county town of Devon with a population of about 102,000. The main part of the city centre includes the High Street and Queen Street where some of the historic parts of the city are located. Prior to 1977, part of the High Street was a dual carriageway and carried large volumes of traffic. Queen Street also suffered the same problems but was further aggravated by the lack of width of both footways and

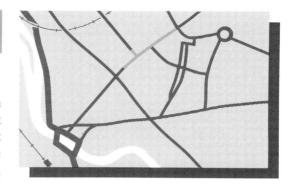

34: The carriageway in High Street narrowed to a single lane primarily for buses. Planted areas in the widened footway add to the appearance and seats allow people to rest and enjoy the surroundings.
(Photo: Devon County Council)

carriageway particularly at the High Street end. Generally, the area suffered from overwhelming domination by motor

34

35

35: Widened footway in Queen Street has improved the area for pedestrians. The flat top hump at footway level assists pedestrians when crossing and the street furniture and planting help define the route traffic has to take. (Photo: Devon County Council)

vehicles which resulted in a hostile and unsafe environment for pedestrians.

OBJECTIVES

The aim was to relieve the problems typical of a city centre, namely intrusion from high volumes of traffic through the main shopping streets and the resulting conflicts in order to stimulate the upgrading of the physical and commercial environment, and to give priority to pedestrians and public transport.

DESCRIPTION

The approach was to introduce pedestrian priority and environmental enhancement in stages. The first stage was implemented in 1977 and included the removal of the former dual carriageway part of the High Street, giving more space to pedestrians by widening of the footways. In the following years further stages were introduced in the High Street and Queen Street, all of which provided further priority and space for the pedestrians.

Road closures and the introduction of traffic management measures enabled all traffic to be excluded from the High Street except for emergency vehicles and buses.

Carriageway narrowing and the creation of better facilities for pedestrians have been provided in Queen Street. A flat top hump has been installed at a very busy pedestrian crossing point to make crossing the road an easier and safer movement. The scheme also involved measures to improve both the functional and aesthetic elements of the streets involved. These included the provision of high quality paving, new and improved street lighting, seats and other street furniture and colour co-ordinated pedestrian finger posts.

COST

The cost was about £250,000.

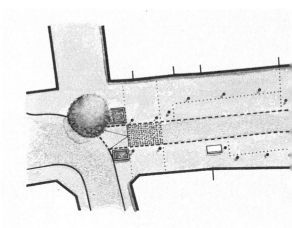

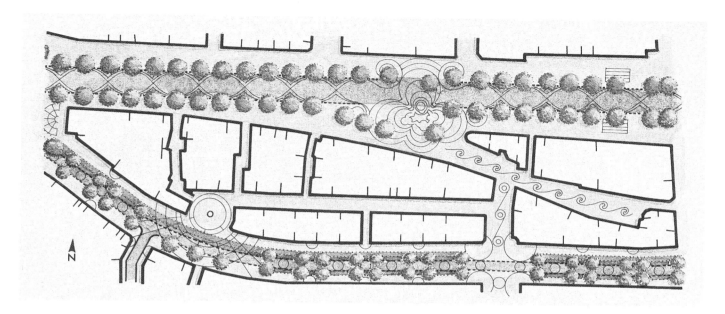

OBJECTIVES

To promote the economic and cultural life of the city by the creation of an attractive city centre, by improving public transport access, and by reducing the speed and volume of motor traffic.

38

39

40: Attention to paving detail and street furniture helps to create a calm yet urban atmosphere in a secondary shopping street in Frankfurt's city centre.
(Photo: T. Pharoah)

40

DESCRIPTION

City centre plans include the removal of vehicles from the most important pedestrian areas and the reduction of traffic impact in other city centre streets by the creation of tree-lined boulevards and "platz". Investment in public transport is a major element of the overall strategy, including "U bahn", "S bahn" and tram developments. Some reduction in parking capacity is also planned.

Major schemes already complete include the pedestrianisation of the main shopping street, Zeil, which formerly carried 35,000 vehicles a day, the conversion to boulevards with restricted carriageways of Rossmarkt, parts of Kaiserstrasse, and other major city centre streets, and the creation of a large traffic-free "platz" around the refurbished opera house.

COST

Not known.

ASSESSMENT

Not known.

41

43

42

41: Reducing traffic space does not have to await costly reconstruction. Here a lane is temporarily closed off with planter boxes.
(Photo: T. Pharoah)

42: Frankfurt's main shopping street, the Zeil, formerly carrying 35,000 vehicles a day and now a haven for pedestrians.
(Photo: T. Pharoah)

43: Removal of traffic lanes allows the creation of a spacious boulevard, which will eventually stretch from the city centre to the main station.
(Photo: T.Pharoah)

44: Plateau at the junction of Fargate and High Street.
(Photo: K. Platt)

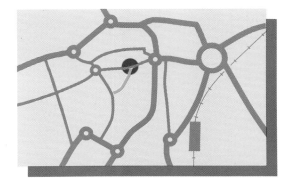

CONTEXT

Fargate is a major city centre shopping street and was the first to be pedestrianised in Sheffield. At its northern end it joins High Street which has a high bus flow and many bus stops. A bus gate (with exemptions) operates near to the junction with Fargate. In this vicinity at peak shopping times about 2,000 pedestrians per hour cross High Street which has a vehicle flow of about 330 per hour, predominantly buses. The pedestrian subway serving this crossing movement was used by only a small proportion of pedestrians, the majority crossing at various surface locations, often between stationary buses, across a carriageway up to 14m wide.

OBJECTIVES

The purpose of the scheme was to replace the little-used pedestrian subway with an attractive and safe surface level alternative. The scheme was designed to encourage pedestrian crossing movements to be concentrated over one short section near the bus gate.

DESCRIPTION

The carriageway in High Street where it passes the end of Fargate was narrowed to 6.4m (still allowing two-way bus flow) and a plateau was formed over the narrowed section. The plateau and approach ramps were constructed using paving blocks. A kerb upstand of 10mm assists certain pedestrian groups while a further distinction between footway and carriageway was achieved by using charcoal coloured blocks on the plateau in contrast to the buff coloured paving in adjacent areas. The ramps were constructed from brindle coloured blocks. The plateau was made as long as practicable, 18m, in order to cater for the volume of pedestrians.

44

45

COST

Not available.

ASSESSMENT

Speed reduction experiments were carried out in conjunction with a bus company to determine the appropriate ramp gradient to raise the carriageway by 100 mm. The "before" free-flowing 85 percentile bus speed was 19.5 mph. The figure decreased to 16.5 mph with ramps constructed at 1 in 17; 14.5 mph at 1 in 13; and surprisingly, 14.5 mph at 1 in 10. The latter gradient did, however, further reduce non-bus speeds, the overall 85 percentile speed reducing from 22 to 17 mph. The carriageway narrowing coupled with a change in horizontal alignment causes two buses to pass extremely slowly, or one to take a central line through the bus gate. Either practice is satisfactory from a pedestrian safety viewpoint. The speed reduction effect of this narrowing is additional to the measured free-flow figures given.

Accident numbers are too small and the "after" period too short for benefits to be

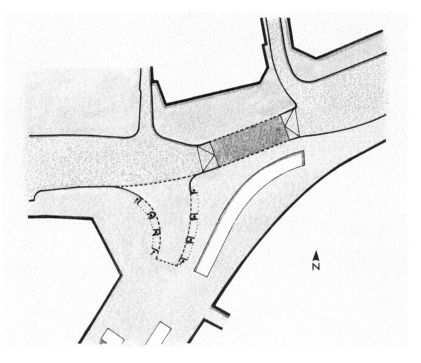

assessed with certainty, but early results are encouraging. Pedestrian accidents at or near the bus gate averaged 3.5 per year (with a fatal/serious/slight injury ratio of 1:5:16), and during the 18 months "after" period there were two slight injury accidents. The number of bus passenger accidents has remained approximately the same.

Early indications are that the main pedestrian flow is now more concentrated at the bus gate and the scheme has created a change in driver behaviour. The impression is that whereas previously a bus at 20 mph would intimidate pedestrians, a driver now approaching at 14 mph will be in a position to appreciate pedestrian difficulties and will often give precedence to them.

45: The narrow carriageway plateau is clearly distinguished from the pedestrian area by a low kerb and different coloured paving. (Photo: K. Platt)

46: Pedestrians enjoy significant benefits from the improved layout and environment. (Photo: Devon County Council)

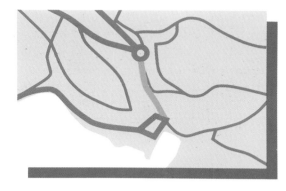

CONTEXT

The scheme was undertaken in parallel with a major shopping redevelopment scheme in Torquay Town Centre. Prior to the new development, known as Fleet Walk, Fleet Street was a somewhat run-down shopping area located between the harbour area and the main shopping area of the town.

OBJECTIVES

The enhancement of Fleet Street was considered by Torbay Borough Council and the County Council to be an integral part of the Fleet Walk development, and the scheme was designed and developed by these authorities in partnership with the developers, Rosehaugh Estates.

46

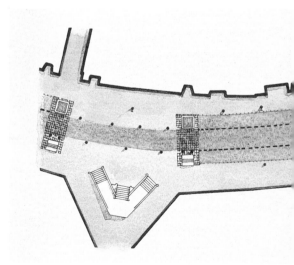

The principal objective of the scheme was to create a pedestrian priority area in the street which would complement the design of the new development at the southern end, and which could be extended to the remainder of the street outside the redevelopment area, at the northern end.

DESCRIPTION

Concrete pavers were laid across the full width of the street which was closed to traffic, with the exception of buses and service vehicles. Other vehicles are permitted outside the hours of 10 a.m. to 6 p.m. for access purposes only. The question of designing a track for these vehicles and of providing service areas where necessary was a matter of considerable debate during the design stages. The arrangement finally adopted used street furniture including bollards, planters and litter bins which were carefully located so as to mark the route for buses and service vehicles.

COST

The scheme was carried out as part of the redevelopment of Fleet Street by a private developer. The cost is estimated at between £0.5m and £0.75m.

47: Paving across the full width of the street. Bollards, planters and other street furniture define the vehicle track. (Photo: Devon County Council)

47

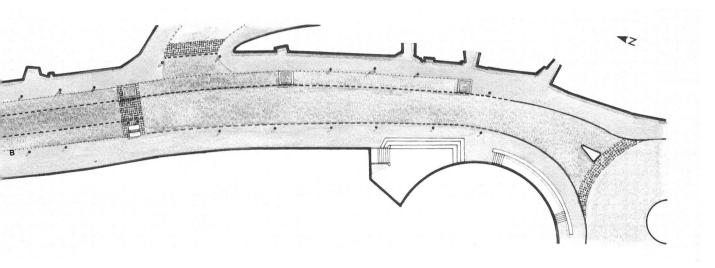

ASSESSMENT

Initially, there were problems of conflict between buses and pedestrians. Approximately 100 minibuses were travelling through the street every hour. However, following discussions with the bus companies, the numbers of vehicles using the street has been reduced and an agreement has been reached which ensures that these vehicles travel at no more than 5 mph. Some amendments to the scheme have been required to calm traffic at the northern end of Fleet Street from which access is required to adjoining streets.

Notwithstanding these initial difficulties, the overall effect of the scheme has been beneficial in terms of improving the environment and safety for shoppers and tourists. The major problem has been the difficulties experienced by people with a visual handicap owing to the absence of kerbs and the location of street furniture and this matter is the subject of further investigation.

CONTEXT

Kalker Strasse is a main radial road on the east side of the Rhine, which acts as an important focus for the suburban community of Kalk with intensive shopping, commercial and apartment uses. Following the opening in 1982 of a new radial road to the north of Kalk, the traffic function of Kalker Strasse was downgraded, and rebuilding was necessary when the street tramway was upgraded to "U bahn" and placed in a cut-and-cover tunnel beneath the street. The street is roughly 26m wide between buildings.

OBJECTIVES

The objective was to exploit the opportunities presented by rebuilding to improve the "town centre" function and character of Kalker Strasse, in conjunction with housing and commercial regeneration work in the Kalk district. This was to be achieved by reducing through traffic and providing greater priority to pedestrians and the so-called "staying" functions of the street.

DESCRIPTION

The former 18m carriageway (including tram tracks) has been reduced to 7m, with one lane in each direction clearly marked. Alternative routes were provided for cyclists. Turning lanes have been retained at major junctions only.

48: The carriageway in Kalker Strasse has been narrowed to a single lane in each direction, providing more space for other purposes. (Photo: T. Pharoah)

An unusual feature is a discontinuous loading lane (2.5 m) provided adjacent to the carriageway. Linear meter-controlled parking has been provided at the side (at footway level). Thus formalised double-parking has been created.

Footways were widened to a minimum of 5m, with further extensions at junctions and at signal controlled crossings.

48

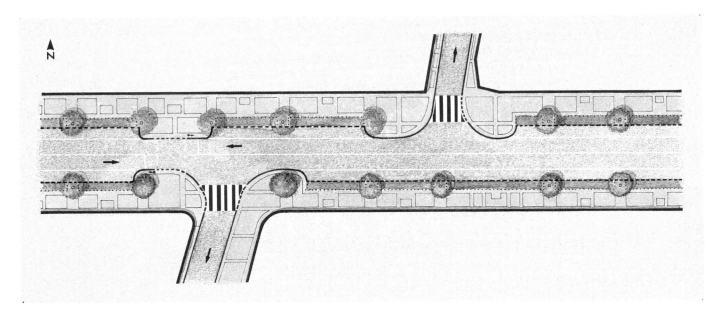

Functional surfacing has been used, with asphalt for the carriageway and loading lane, and concrete tile paving elsewhere. Accentuation of the "place" has been achieved through ornamentation of the side areas and trees planted between parking spaces. The loading lane is designed to be formally (aesthetically) in the carriageway, while the parking spaces are formally part of the side (footway) areas.

Separate lighting has been provided for the carriageway and side areas, the latter being on short standards and designed to be sympathetic to the pedestrian scale and atmosphere.

Infill developments in the frontage have been designed to provide new pedestrian access ways to renovated housing areas to the rear. Pedestrian crossings are located to coincide with these access ways.

COST

The scheme was part of the works related to upgrading the tram system, and relocating the tracks under Kalker Strasse. The cost of the traffic calming works cannot be separately identified.

ASSESSMENT

An improvement of the "town centre" atmosphere has been achieved with the building developments and a "boulevard" character has been created by the extension and ornamentation of the side (pedestrian) spaces.

Through traffic has been reduced from 27,000 to 13,000 vehicles per day.

The intensive function-mixing has led to some speed reduction in the street, especially during shopping hours when it is most beneficial.

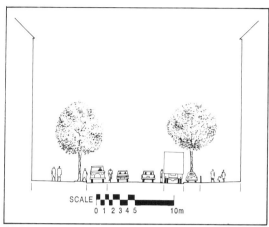

CROSS SECTION OF FOOTWAY AND CARRIAGEWAY

49

As the loading lane is part of the traffic space, it is accepted and obvious that it is for short-stay only. The carriageway is clearly "outside" the pedestrian space but crossing still presents problems. All pedestrian crossings are light controlled, but are too widely spaced (up to 130 m) to prevent some pedestrians crossing at intermediate points. Accident trends have been rather disappointing and are the subject of continuing study.

The appearance and furnishing of the side areas encourages pedestrians to stay/rest in the street, rather than just hurry through as before.

50

49: Former carriageway converted to a broad pedestrian area with seating, trees, cycle racks and other features which help people to enjoy the street. (Photo: T. Pharoah)

50: Footways are extended at light-controlled pedestrian crossings. The short-term waiting lane between the meter-parking area and the carriageway can also be seen. (Photo: T. Pharoah)

**51: The kerb line of the original 16m wide carriageway is just visible. Within this space can now be seen a narrow carriageway, separate service road, linear parking, extended footways at corners and trees planted to soften the scene.
(Photo: T. Pharoah)**

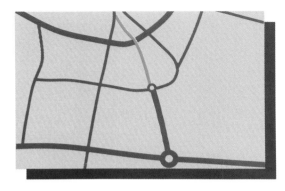

EINDHOVEN · LEENDERWEG NETHERLANDS

CONTEXT

Leenderweg is a main radial route between the inner and middle ring roads of this medium-sized town, with no alternative route for through traffic. "Rat running" traffic on adjacent roads has been stopped and is now accommodated on this route. Suburban shopping and commercial activities occur along most of the road, together with housing. Buildings are of medium density and height. It is a bus route with 6 to 10 buses per hour each way. The scheme was carried out as part of the Eindhoven national traffic calming demonstration project.

OBJECTIVES

The objectives were to reconcile the through traffic function of the street (to be increased with closure of adjacent "rat runs") with its role as a sub centre, and to provide a better environment as well as provision for parking, loading, pedestrians and cyclists.

DESCRIPTION

The approach was to reduce the carriageway (as much as 16m wide in places) to a single lane in each direction and to allocate the resulting space to other activities in the street. Traffic capacity has been maintained by retaining turning lanes at major junctions. The reallocation of street space varies along the length of the street according to the type and intensity of frontage activity. The design measures for the section with the most intensive shopping include:

- A parallel service and parking road with a "Woonerf" atmosphere
- Wider (2.5m) footways, and separate (2.1 m) cycleways

51

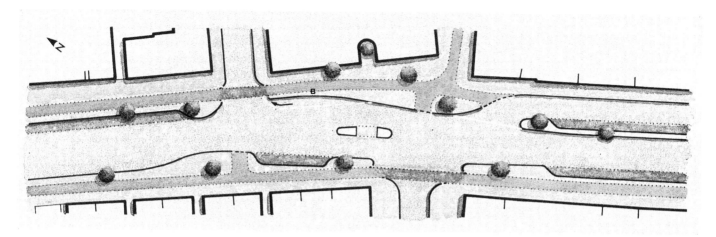

52

- Light controlled pedestrian crossings and central islands of 1.8m width
- Functional surfacing including asphalt for the main carriageway, bricks for the service road, and small concrete tiles for the footways, loading areas and cycleways, the latter in a different colour
- Tree planting on the strip dividing the service road and main carriageway

COST

The cost was £320,000 for the 0.5 km length.

ASSESSMENT

Additional through traffic has not been significant. The supply of on-street parking has been slightly increased and loading is better organised (less double-parking). The new service road has been problem-free, though shoppers are still exposed to the adverse effects of parking activity. The reduced carriageway width has moderated driving speeds, and made crossing easier for pedestrians. The footway and cycleway widths correspond well with the relative demand. The introduction of trees has softened the street scene.

52: A central island shelters turning vehicles. The turning lane on the far side doubles as a bus lay-by. (Photo: T. Pharoah)

53: Coloured bricks are used within parking bays and for the strip which separates them from the main carriageway. Note also the tree planted within the bay, protected by bollards and cast iron grille. (Photo: T. Pharoah)

54: Narrow (6.5 m) carriageway and half-width bus lay-by. (Photo: D. Turner)

55: Side road treatment showing footway extensions which define parking bays and provide space for tree planting. The raised carriageway, in small granite setts, provides a level pedestrian crossing. Cast iron bollards keep vehicles off the footway. (Photo: D. Turner)

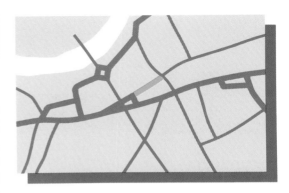

WANDSWORTH
ST JOHN'S HILL

CONTEXT

St. John's Hill is a busy inner London street with mixed shopping and commercial use near Clapham Junction railway station. It lies between and parallel to the A3 trunk road and the A3205, both of which are main radial roads. It is an important bus route with 37 buses per hour in each direction. Traffic flows during the morning peak are in excess of 2,000 vehicles per hour (two way). The carriageway had previously been marked out for one traffic lane in each direction divided by a 2.5m central strip with hatched markings, and incorporating 1.8m wide islands.

OBJECTIVES

The aims were: to reduce traffic speeds, which were reported to be excessive in the off-peak evening period; to prevent vehicles parking in the central hatched area; and to discourage use of the street as a through route. The scheme was also designed to

53

54

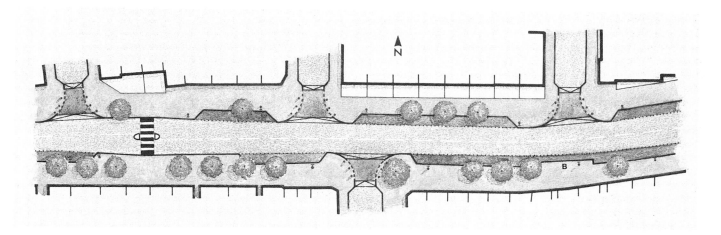

improve the environment of the street, especially for pedestrians.

DESCRIPTION

The carriageway has been narrowed to 6.5m, except at zebra crossings where central islands are provided. Parking bays on either side are defined by footway extensions where parking is undesirable, namely at junctions and near pedestrian crossings. Half-width bus bays have been incorporated to allow at least smaller vehicles to pass stationary buses. The parking bays are defined also by the use of brick paving, and are separated from the carriageway by a narrow strip of bricks in a different colour. These strips provide some space to help parking manoeuvres, the opening of car doors, and extra room for cyclists.

The entrances to all side roads have been ramped and raised to footway height to reduce the speed of turning vehicles and to provide a level crossing facility for pedestrians. Vehicles are prevented from straying onto footway areas by substantial cast iron bollards. Corner radii have been given fairly generous dimensions to prevent delays on the main road caused by vehicles waiting to turn.

55

56

56: Wider and repaved
footways provide a more
attractive setting for the
cafe tables.
(Photo: D. Turner)

Environmental improvements include repaving of footway areas, tree planting and new lighting. Some hanging baskets and other street furnishings have been provided with sponsorship by commercial interests in the street.

COST

The cost was £440,000 excluding the design and supervision of the scheme.

ASSESSMENT

The scheme was completed in September 1990. Conversations with people in the street, including some property owners, revealed positive attitudes to the environmental improvements.

BARNSTAPLE
BOUTPORT STREET

CONTEXT

Boutport Street is one of the major town centre shopping and commercial streets in Barnstaple. It was also a primary county route carrying a heavy volume of through traffic in addition to substantial local traffic flows. There was an urgent need for environmental and safety improvements for pedestrians particularly at the crossing points along this street.

OBJECTIVES

The main objectives of the scheme were to reduce traffic flows to access only, to widen the footways and to provide crossing points at footway level for pedestrians.

DESCRIPTION

The completion of a relief road provided the opportunity for the introduction of traffic calming measures which included:
- Traffic Orders and carriageway alterations restricting access to buses and loading only on sections of the street
- Road narrowing by means of walled planters with crossing points at footway level
- Widening of the footways

COST

The cost was £65,000.

57: Carriageway constriction with pedestrian crossing at footway level. The layout is defined by the use of raised planter beds and street furniture. (Photo: Devon County Council)

ASSESSMENT

By routeing traffic along the Relief Road, traffic flow in Boutport Street has been reduced considerably. In certain sections of the street traffic is restricted to access only. This, together with the widening of the footways, has improved the environment for shoppers and enhanced the street scene generally.

57

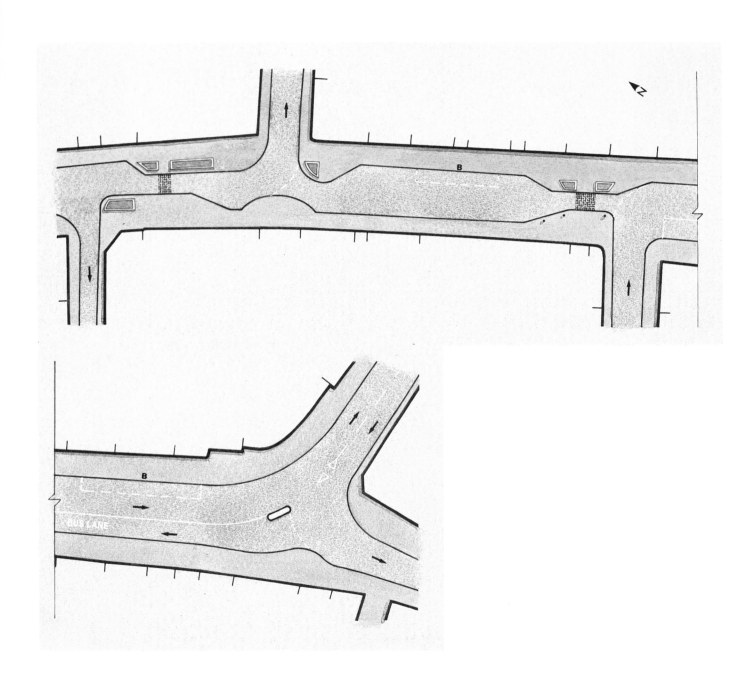

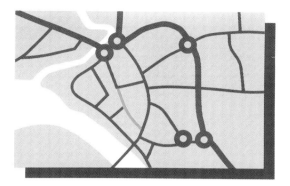

58

CONTEXT

The High Street is a busy main shopping street, narrow in places, and is the focus of pedestrian activity in Barnstaple. Conflict between vehicular traffic and pedestrians was severe and environmental conditions were of unacceptable standards.

OBJECTIVES

The main objectives were: to exclude traffic from the High Street, except for access for goods vehicles, during most of the working day; to introduce measures to reduce traffic speeds at other times; and to implement environmental improvements.

DESCRIPTION

Traffic in the middle section of the High Street is excluded from 9.15 a.m. to 5 p.m. with access for goods vehicles only at other times. The footways have been widened and the carriageway surfaced with clay pavers and removable bollards have been installed

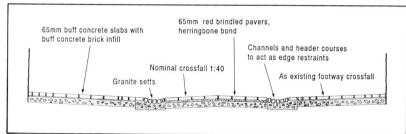

65mm buff concrete slabs with buff concrete brick infill

65mm red brindled pavers, herringbone bond

Channels and header courses to act as edge restraints

Nominal crossfall 1:40

As existing footway crossfall

Granite setts

TYPICAL CROSS SECTION

at each end. Access to the northern section of the High Street is also restricted to vehicles loading and unloading only, Monday to Friday 8 a.m. to 6 p.m. and is open to pedestrians only on Saturdays.

COST

The cost of the paving was £40,000 and that for narrowing the carriageway £1,000 which was paid by developers.

58: Full width paving enhances the street scene. Vehicle speeds have been reduced during the times when access is allowed. (Photo: Devon County Council)

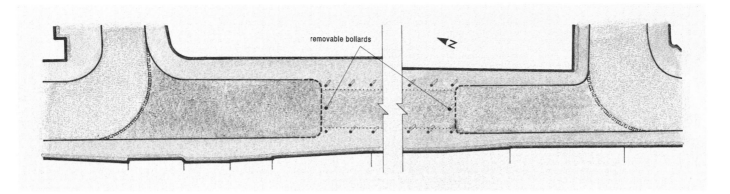

ASSESSMENT

There has been a positive improvement in the shopping environment of the High Street with considerable benefits to the comfort and safety of pedestrians. Disabled drivers have also benefited from the scheme as they are exempted from the restrictions to vehicles loading and unloading in the northern section of the High Street.

It is proposed to fully pedestrianise the northern end of High Street and to extend the partial pedestrianisation to the other main town centre shopping streets.

CONTEXT

Tuly Street is a busy town centre street serving amongst other things a large car park. Traffic speeds were too high particularly at busy pedestrian crossing points with inadequate visibility.

OBJECTIVES

The aim was to slow the traffic to an acceptable level compatible with the street's function as an access road and a busy pedestrian link.

DESCRIPTION

The following measures were introduced:

• Footways were widened on both sides to create a "throttle" only 3m wide, negotiable by one vehicle at a time

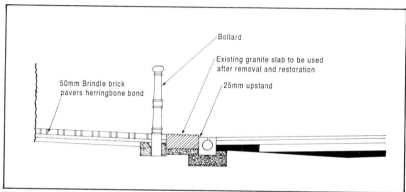

TYPICAL CROSS SECTION OF FOOTWAY

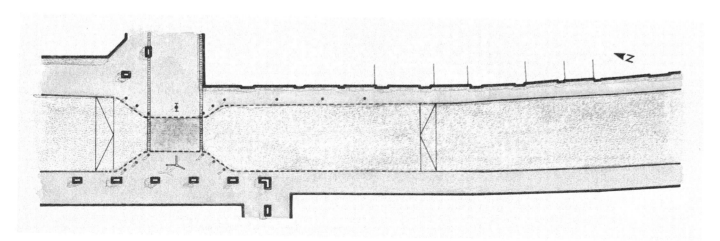

59

- A flat top hump/pedestrian crossing was constructed
- New street furniture was provided, such as cast iron bollards, fingerposts and ornate lamp columns

COST

The cost was estimated at £3,000 and met by developers.

ASSESSMENT

The scheme has achieved the objectives by being very effective in reducing traffic speeds and making it easier and safer for pedestrians to cross the street.

CONTEXT

Borehamwood lies to the north of Greater London some 8 km east of Watford. The last period of major growth occurred after the second world war when Borehamwood was chosen as a location for London overspill housing. The rapid influx of new residents in the 1950s resulted in pressure for shopping development, and Shenley Road became the main shopping street.

The town centre has no areas of outstanding townscape. On the whole the architecture is of poor standard and the layout is monotonous. Together with traffic congestion, parked cars and street clutter, Shenley Road offered a poor environment for all users.

OBJECTIVES

Since 1987 considerable efforts by the Hertsmere Borough Council and Hertfordshire County Council have been applied to the design of a Town Centre Enhancement Scheme for Shenley Road. The main problem which thwarted progress on proposals was the volume of traffic which Shenley Road carries, some 18,000 vehicles per day.

With no opportunities to divert this traffic onto alternative routes, and no space to create a bypass, any scheme would therefore have to accommodate this high volume of traffic.

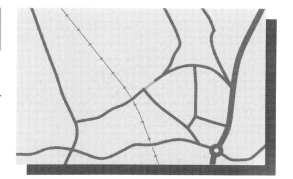

60

The initial objectives of enhancement were seen in terms of traffic conditions in Shenley Road. Firstly, considerable illegal parking "cluttered" the street, created difficulties for pedestrians, and reduced road capacity. Secondly, the aim was to lower vehicle speeds in order to reduce noise, fumes, and the probability of accidents. Thirdly, by maintaining a regular but slower flow of traffic, congestion at peak times could be avoided.

60: Flat top hump to slow traffic and help pedestrians cross, combined with a narrow carriageway and wide central island. A lateral shift has been created with a servicing bay (foreground).
(Photo: T. Pharoah)

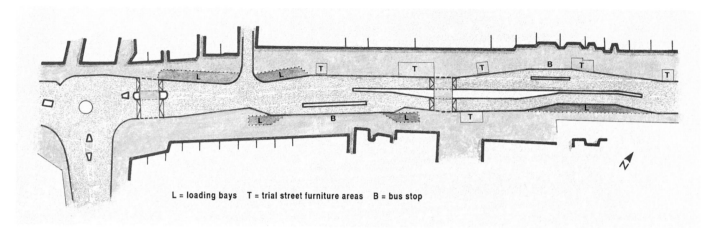

L = loading bays   T = trial street furniture areas   B = bus stop

61

61: Mini roundabout replacing traffic signals at the start of the treated section of Shenley Road. A wider central refuge has also been provided. (Photo: T. Pharoah)

DESCRIPTION

In 1989, officers from Hertfordshire County Council and Hertsmere Borough Council visited Langenfeld in Germany where problems similar to those in Borehamwood had been tackled (see Langenfeld example). One major difference was that Shenley Road carries almost twice the volume of traffic of that in Langenfeld's main street. For this reason it was proposed to implement an experimental scheme over part of Shenley Road using low cost materials. A multi-disciplinary team was set up consisting of both Borough and County Council officers. The features of the scheme were designed with the high flow of traffic in mind, and included the following:-

- Provision of a central island, reducing the width of the carriageway to 3.6m in places, with the aim of reducing traffic speed, providing a refuge for pedestrians, and eliminating illegal parking (reinforced by a legal ban)
- Provision of road crossing points using flat top humps to slow traffic and emphasize the presence of pedestrians
- Modification of bus lay-bys to discourage illegal parking by other vehicles
- Removal of traffic lights at two principal junctions and replacement by mini roundabouts, to allow a smooth flow of traffic at lower speed

The use of these traffic calming measures with relatively high traffic flows was breaking new ground, and it was therefore decided that this jointly led scheme would run for an experimental six month period to allow time for modifications and assessment.

Public consultation was seen as a priority. Publicity leaflets were produced and an exhibition describing the aims of the scheme and proposals toured local offices, schools and community centres. Information posters were distributed advising people on how the new features should be used, including encouragement to use the town centre car parks. "Sharing our Environment" became the slogan used on advertising material along with a logo specifically designed for the scheme.

In addition, an Action Group was set up which consists of representatives from the local community, Town Council, Chamber of Commerce, bus operators, people with disabilities, and other interested groups. The Action Group works with the design team, commenting on the work so far, and providing up-dates on the day to day running of the scheme.

62

63

62: Flat top hump at busiest pedestrian crossing point, showing broad central island and ramp markings. (Photo: T. Pharoah)

63: One of the paving and street furniture test areas, adjacent to a flat top hump crossing area. (Photo: T. Pharoah)

COST

Not relevant at experimental stage.

ASSESSMENT

Before implementation and during the experimental period, monitoring of Shenley Road and other roads in the vicinity was undertaken. Pedestrian movement, parking and servicing were studied and street interviews were carried out to gain public opinion on the shopping centre as a whole. There is a marked improvement in the treated part of Shenley Road. Pedestrians move more freely and with greater confidence as the traffic flows more evenly at much reduced speeds. As the scheme has proved successful it is to be extended.

To assist in the selection of surface materials and street furniture when the scheme is implemented on a permanent basis, various manufacturers donated paving materials, seats and litter bins. These have been used in test areas within pedestrian spaces and are being assessed for wear and tear, staining and discolouration.

At the end of 1990, the permanent scheme was in the process of being designed as the experimental scheme continued to function. The proposed use of high quality materials, redesign of the existing lighting scheme, new landscaping and co-ordinated street furniture will bring style to the town centre. This, along with the slow and steady movement of traffic, will help to create a place for people to visit, stop and enjoy.

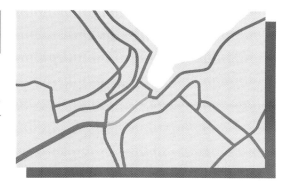

CONTEXT

Brixham is one of Devon's most popular tourist resorts, attracting a large number of visitors during the summer months. Fore Street is the main shopping street. To reduce the risk of conflict with vehicles and improve comfort for pedestrians a seasonal pedestrian priority scheme was introduced in 1971. However, this arrangement offered little scope to improve the appearance of the area and to enhance the environment for shoppers and tourists.

OBJECTIVES

The Local Plan advocated the development of two distributor roads to the north and south of the town centre. The aim was to exploit this opportunity to extend the seasonal pedestrian priority in Fore Street

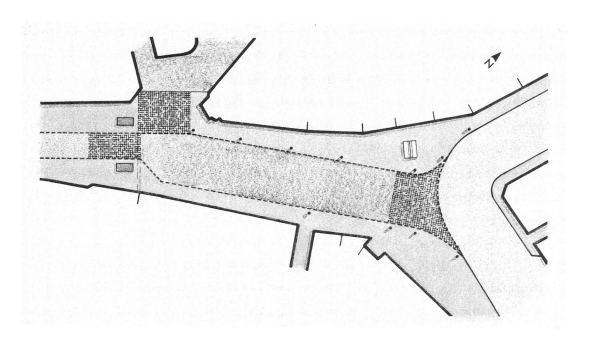

64

64: Carriageway and footways paved at one level. Contrasting colours define the vehicle track.
(Photo: Devon County Council)

COST

The cost was £214,000.

ASSESSMENT

Early signs indicate that the scheme has had a positive effect on pedestrian safety and comfort. The new enhanced street scene has proved to be popular with residents, visitors and the traders. A full assessment of the scheme is not yet available.

from 5 months only to all the year round and to implement functional and environmental improvements to help revitalise the shopping street and enhance its character. This was to be achieved by excluding traffic between 10 a.m. and 6 p.m. from Fore Street together with its complete reconstruction with high quality materials.

DESCRIPTION

Traffic Orders were made in respect of the extension of the summertime pedestrian priority in Fore Street to 12 months of the year, to enable the reconstruction of the street to take place. The former carriageway and footways were paved at one level. The "vehicle track" was defined by brick pavers in a contrasting colour. A comprehensive range of street furniture was provided as well as new street lighting and some feature planting which includes seating.

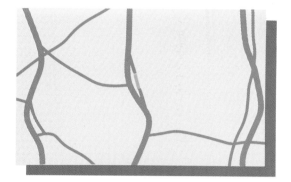

CONTEXT

Buntingford is a small Hertfordshire town about 50 km north of London. It was chosen for the County's first Town Centre Enhancement scheme because of the range of problems experienced in the High Street, and opportunities for their solution. Prior to the opening of a bypass in June 1987, Buntingford High Street carried the A10 trunk road traffic. This created particular problems because the High Street is very narrow (11m - 14m between the buildings) and contains many historic buildings in commercial and residential use. The problems were further compounded by a high proportion of heavy goods vehicles, associated with a large distribution depot to the south of the town.

OBJECTIVES

The opening of the bypass created a number of opportunities and problems in the town centre. Traffic had been reduced but traffic speeds had significantly increased, while some through traffic still used the High Street. Years of being pounded by trunk road traffic had left the street in a state of environmental neglect. Pedestrians were faced with narrow and uneven footways, and the High Street did not offer a proper setting for its fine historic buildings. At the same time, traders feared that a loss of business would result from the removal of through traffic. The objective of the scheme was therefore to exploit the environmental and

65: Buntingford High Street before the opening of the bypass in 1987.
(Photo: Hertfordshire County Council)

66: The traffic calmed High Street showing repaved and wider footways, and narrow section of carriageway at a flat top hump.
(Photo: Hertfordshire County Council)

65

66

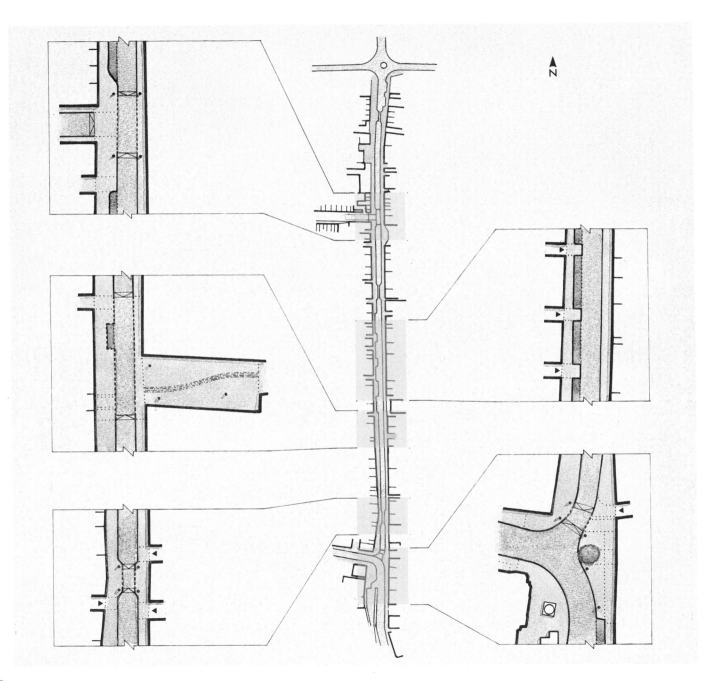

67

68

commercial opportunities while solving the remaining traffic problems in the street.

DESCRIPTION

The design concept incorporated lessons learnt from a study tour to ten towns in The Netherlands and Germany during 1987, and emphasized measures to calm traffic without excluding it altogether, a comprehensive approach to design, and extensive public participation. It was recognised that the scheme should not just slow the speed of traffic, but should also introduce extensive environmental improvements.

To slow vehicle speeds the carriageway was reduced to 4.8m, a width which allows a car and a lorry to pass each other with care. To reduce the need for two lorries to pass in the street, a weight limit of 5 tonnes was imposed on south-bound vehicles. Additional speed controls were introduced using flat top humps (carriageway raised to footway height) and carriageway constrictions with a width of 3m. These

devices were placed at intervals along the street and allow only single file traffic.

To slow vehicles entering the High Street the junctions were substantially altered. At the southern end priority was changed so that vehicles have to make a definite turn at a give-way junction. At the northern end a mini roundabout was introduced and the carriageway was narrowed and offset. These changes have also helped to close long views down the High Street.

Parking bays paved with blocks were provided and these are defined by kerbing and extensions to accessways (crossovers) at footway height. Footways have been widened by up to 1m on either side at the southern end of the street. The junction with Church Street is a focal point in the High Street where special environmental treatment was justified. A level wall-to-wall

67: "Before" situation at the south end of the High Street. (Photo: Hertfordshire County Council)

68: "After" situation at the south end of the High Street showing realignment and change of traffic priority, and enlarged pedestrian area outside public house with seating and planting. (Photo: Hertfordshire County Council)

69: "Before" arrangement at the north end of the High Street. (Photo: Hertfordshire County Council)

70: North end of the High Street showing realignment and narrowing of the carriageway, flat top hump in brick, and new planted areas. (Original centre line markings are just visible). (Photo: Hertfordshire County Council)

71: Detail of a carriageway constriction in the High Street showing area raised to footway level and vertical definition provided by cast iron bollards and a litter bin. (Photo: Hertfordshire County Council)

72: "Before" situation where Church Street joins the High Street. (Photo: Hertfordshire County Council)

69

70

71

surface was built using high quality materials (York stone and granite), with the purpose of creating an attractive pedestrian environment.

The co-ordinated design and environmental enhancements include the removal of telegraph and lighting poles, new street lights attached to buildings, planting, and quality cast-iron bollards. Surfaces include coloured carriageway, textured concrete paving tiles and uncut small cobbles for edging details. Attempts were also made to reduce the number and prominence of traffic signs and markings.

The scheme involved joint working between officers from the County's Highways and Planning Departments. Under the leadership of a Group Engineer there was a design team of engineers skilled in construction, lighting and safety together with planners, architects and landscape architects. The purpose was to achieve a design with integrated traffic and environmental measures. The details of the design were developed at a scale of 1:20, and this enabled problems to be resolved on paper rather than during construction.

Public consultation was extensive. In addition to leaflets and public meetings, four public exhibitions were mounted and an Action Group was set up to provide the designers with feedback. The Action Group consists of representatives from the local community (Town Council, Civic Society, Chamber of Commerce, Police and District Council) and has met regularly since 1987. The availability of staff at a project office established in the High Street during construction also helped to achieve public acceptance of the scheme.

72

73

74

COST

The cost of the main contract covering 600m of the High Street was about £400,000 excluding planning and design work. Planning began in 1987 and the main construction contract lasted 18 weeks from July to December 1989. Further surface improvements carried out during 1990 were financed by the District Council.

ASSESSMENT

"After" studies were not complete at the time of writing, but traffic speeds appear to have been reduced, and the street atmosphere has changed from a traffic corridor to a focal point for this small Hertfordshire town. Parking problems have been reduced, for example the extended footways have discouraged cars from obstructing accessways. Commercial faith in the High Street appears to have been increased, with many shopkeepers and residents improving their properties.

75

73: Church Street after redesign as a pedestrian priority area, paved from wall to wall in York stone. The granite gulley provides a guide for vehicles passing through. Part of the High Street block paving can be seen in the foreground. (Photo: Hertfordshire County Council)

74: Small cobbles provide a neat setting for cast iron bollards. (Photo: T. Pharoah)

75: Victorian-style wall-mounted lighting adds visual interest and reduces clutter in the street. (Photo: Hertfordshire County Council)

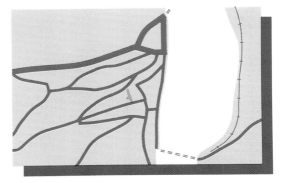

CONTEXT

Dartmouth is an attractive historic town overlooking the River Dart in South Devon. The town centre is recognised as having an outstanding conservation area worthy of special attention to safeguard its future character. In order to provide a framework for the future conservation of this historic settlement a Conservation Area Management Plan was prepared.

OBJECTIVES

The plan, prepared in 1985, concentrated in particular on the townscape of the area between Bayards Cove and the Market Square. The scope of the plan covered the treatment of existing and proposed roads and footways, the control of on-street parking and the appropriateness of different forms of street furniture including traffic signs and street lighting.

DESCRIPTION

The first scheme to be implemented as part of the Management Plan saw the repaving of Foss Street and Union Street. Access to these streets was already limited but it was as a result of the enhancement works that the full potential was realised. The scheme involved repaving the carriageway and footways at one level using traditional yellow and blue brick pavers. Removable bollards placed at the ends of the streets enforce the pedestrian priority. A further extension of the treatment into the adjoining Flavel Street is also programmed.

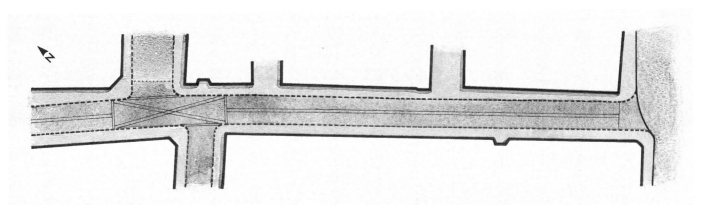

COST

The total cost for Foss Street and Union Street was £25,000.

ASSESSMENT

The scheme undertaken in Foss Street has transformed the appearance of this relatively narrow street into a very attractive place in which to dwell and shop. The business community in the area has responded to improve the appearance even further by the introduction of many flower planters and hanging baskets. This combination of hard and soft landscaping has produced an environment where vehicles are viewed as an intrusion into pedestrian activity.

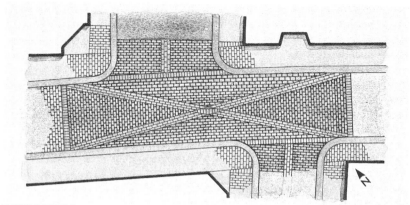

PAVING DETAIL

76

76: The carriageway and footway paved at one level. Traffic is calmed by the overall impression given by the layout of this street. (Photo: Devon County Council)

77: General view of Frankfurter Strasse, Hennef, showing central strip to provide "flexibility" within the narrow carriageway. The lighting adds a distinctive character while the stone plinths provide "shelter" for pedestrians crossing. (Photo: T. Pharoah)

78: Shoppers and more vulnerable cyclists can use the advisory cycleway adjacent to the footway, as shown here. (Photo: T. Pharoah)

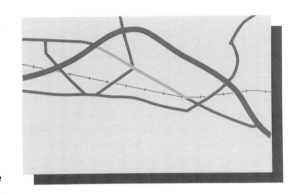

HENNEF · FRANKFURTER STRASSE · GERMANY

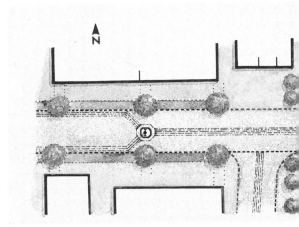

CONTEXT

Hennef is a small town about 10 km east of Bonn. In 1986 the main street, Frankfurter Strasse was relieved of its through traffic function by the opening of the new A560 autobahn to the north, though traffic volumes remain fairly high at 1000 - 1300 vehicles per hour.

OBJECTIVES

The scheme was designed to take the opportunity of creating a safer and more pleasant environment for those using the various facilities in Frankfurter Strasse. The design was to reflect the differing character

77

78

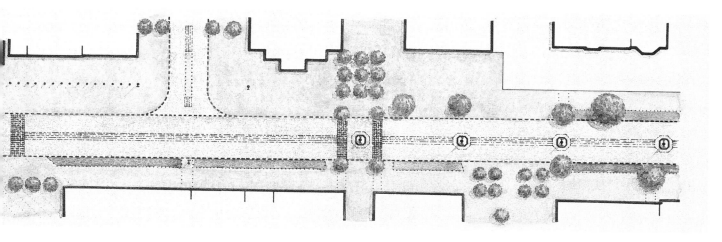

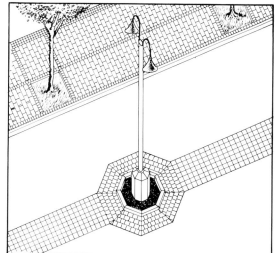

LAMPSTAND AND OCCASIONAL STRIP

79

of the "entrance" areas, an historical farm area, and a commercial core area. The latter area was to be designed to resolve problems arising from intense overlapping of legitimate street activities (shopping, loading, crossing, walking, cycling, access, etc.).

DESCRIPTION

The most important elements of the overall design concerned the shopping and commercial section of the street. The carriageway was reduced in width and divided by a new central strip, paved in granite. The central strip incorporates raised

79: Parking bays are defined by planted areas with low granite borders and protected by stout wooden bollards.
(Photo: T. Pharoah)

80

COST

Not known.

ASSESSMENT

Average traffic speeds have been reduced by 4 mph and the proportion of vehicles travelling in excess of 20 mph through the shopping area has reduced from 63% to 30%.

islands containing a double-light column set in a stone plinth. These plinths create a safe "shadow" area either side where pedestrians crossing the road are shielded from vehicles. The carriageway in each direction is 3.25m wide, but the granite paved strip creates an optical width of 2.8m. Where there is insufficient street width, a single carriageway of about 6m is provided with 1m wide granite strips either side. Parking is in defined bays at footway level. Cyclists are provided with a choice of an "advisory" cycleway within the footway (defined by red paving) or use of the main carriageway. The overall appearance of the street has been enhanced with the use of high quality materials, lighting columns and tree and other planting. The speed limit was reduced from 30 mph to 25 mph.

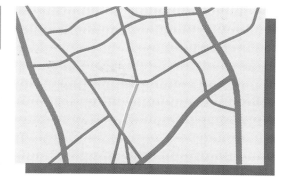

CONTEXT

Langenfeld is a town of about 50,000 inhabitants between Cologne and Dusseldorf. The Hauptstrasse, or "main street", is the shopping and commercial centre and carries about 10,000 motor vehicles and 3,000 cycles per day as well as buses. Although it is a Lander (third tier) road, nearby autobahns mean that most of the traffic is generated by the town itself. The street is 1.2 km long.

OBJECTIVES

The street had a concentration of accidents, estimated to cost £500,000 per year, and traffic conditions generally created a poor environment for shoppers. The fairly straight and open aspect, with a carriageway width of up to 14m encouraged excessive driving speeds. The aim was therefore to reduce accidents while making the street more pleasant and convenient to use.

DESCRIPTION

The adopted scheme combines a number of measures to slow vehicle speeds and to make it easier for pedestrians to cross the street. Speed reduction is mainly achieved using cushions and to a lesser extent lateral shifts. The shifts have also allowed tree planting in a way which shortens the driver's forward view. Central islands with pedestrian crossing places

81: Cyclists are provided with a separate path to reduce conflict on the narrow carriageway. Although safer for cyclists, conflicts can arise with pedestrians and bus passengers at busy locations where space is scarce.
(Photo: T. Pharoah)

82: Lateral carriageway shift produced by alternate build-out and central island. Cyclists are provided with a separate path at footway level but separated by lighting columns and a change of surface colour. Trees help to screen parked cars.
(Photo: T. Pharoah)

81

82

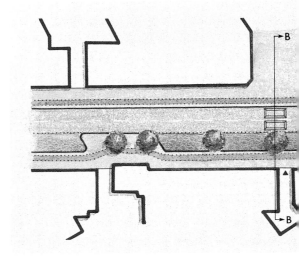

83

83: Central islands with areas flush with the carriageway help pedestrians to cross and provide "shelter" for turning vehicles.
(Photo: T. Pharoah)

84/85: The carriageway alignment at this bus stop allows vehicles to pass, but makes it easy for the bus to rejoin the stream when ready. Note that the pedestrian crossing is defined with coloured bricks rather than paint.
(Photo: T. Pharoah)

84

85

alternate with footway extensions and car parking, thus creating the lateral shifts. Separate cycleways have also been provided adjacent to or within the footway. Bus stops are designed to give priority to buses, either by preventing other vehicles from overtaking, or by giving immediate access back into the traffic queue. The cushions are 1.6m wide which allows buses to pass over

them unaffected. Footways and cycleways are continued at the same level across side road junctions. A speed limit of 25 mph applies. The carriageway has been reduced in width, though not to the extent desired because of requirements laid down by the military authorities.

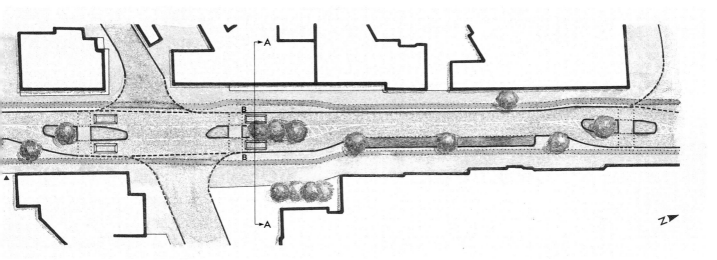

COST

Not known.

ASSESSMENT

Traffic speeds have been reduced to below 25 mph in the vicinity of the cushions. These are effective in encouraging drivers to stop for pedestrians at crossing places, especially those placed in advance of the crossing. Parking in the defined on-street spaces interrupts traffic flow and so also helps to keep speeds down. Crossing the street has been made easier for pedestrians, though they do not always use the specially designed crossing places. Planting at the side and in the central islands has softened the appearance of the street.

Pedestrians do not always respect the cycleways which causes some friction, but not danger. It would seem that the side road junctions have over-generous dimensions which means that pedestrians and cyclists

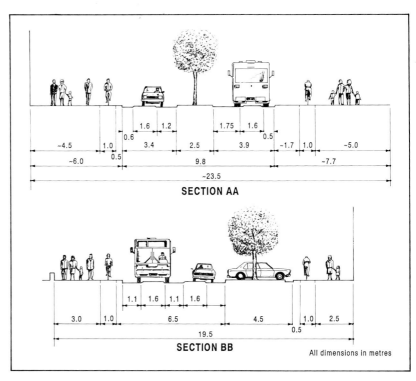

SECTION AA

SECTION BB

All dimensions in metres

86: Cushions are of limited width so that buses can pass over without discomfort to passengers.
(Photo: T. Pharoah)

87: A cushion immediately before a crossing encourages drivers to give way to pedestrians.
(Photo: T. Pharoah)

88: Central island provided at a pedestrian crossing and bus stops. Other vehicles cannot overtake a bus at the stop, and are slowed by a cushion. Note also planting on the central island, the lateral shift further ahead, the separate cycleway, the use of colour to define side roads (foreground) and footways, and the reminder 40 kph (25 mph) speed limit sign.
(Photo: T. Pharoah)

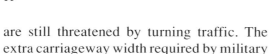

86

87

are still threatened by turning traffic. The extra carriageway width required by military traffic in the north-bound direction has meant an over-large gap between the cushions and the kerb which allows drivers of smaller cars to avoid the cushions.

The accident and other research results are not yet available.

88

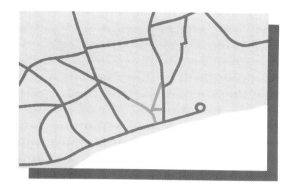

CONTEXT

Sidmouth is an historic settlement of national importance. The town centre is recognised as one of the most significant Conservation Areas within Devon. Whilst much had been done to protect this heritage there were areas within the town centre where positive measures were needed to improve the appearance of the centre as a whole.

OBJECTIVES

The aim was to undertake enhancement work, including the treatment of roads and footways and the provision of appropriate forms of street furniture and lighting. Proposals included possible removal, relocation or replacement of unsympathetic road signs.

DESCRIPTION

Detailed treatments were prepared and have been implemented for a number of the town centre streets. Old Fore Street and Market Square/Prospect Place have been paved at one level using brick sized pavers. Traffic is restricted in Old Fore Street to permit holders and service vehicles only and on-street parking has been removed.

In New Street and Church Street brick sized pavers have again been used, however a kerb has been retained and the carriageway defined in a different colour from the footways as the route is used for local traffic.

Some on-street parking has been retained, although in New Street this has been restricted to disabled badge holders only. In addition, to mark the entrance to the town centre, a flat top hump has been introduced in High Street near the junction with All Saints Road.

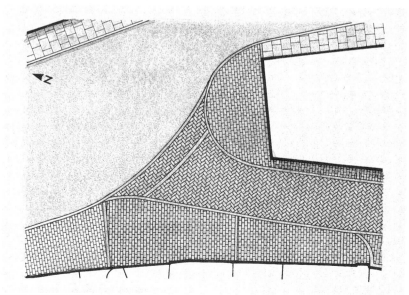

SURFACE DETAIL AT JUNCTION

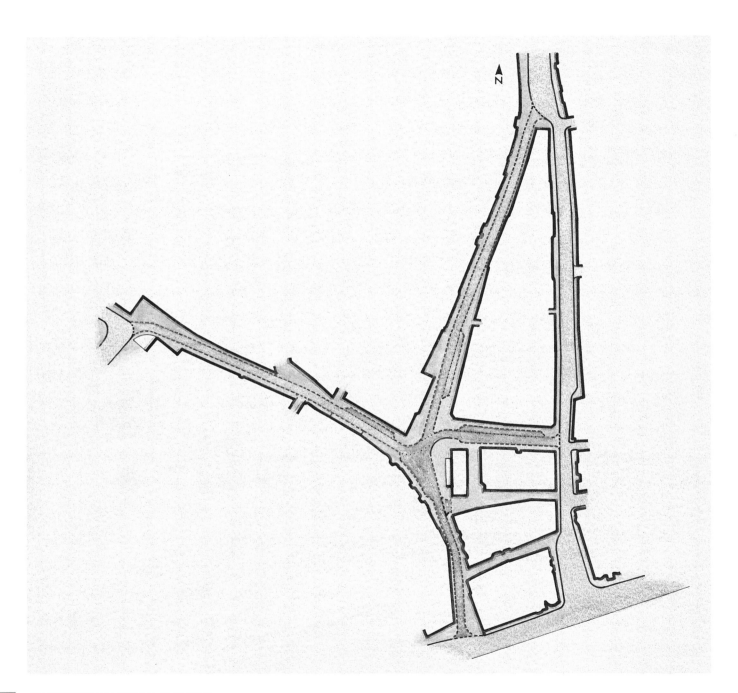

COST

The cost was in the region of £400,000.

ASSESSMENT

The scheme has resulted in a reduction of vehicles using these important shopping streets. The traffic restrictions now in force in Old Fore Street result in the street being pedestrianised for much of the day; this is particularly important during the summer when considerable numbers of tourists visit this attractive Regency town.

89

89: Brick sized pavers laid at one level create a shared-surface street. (Photo: Devon County Council)

90: The Wills Memorial Island. The paving and footway widening has helped to reduce vehicle speeds and provided a safer and pleasanter area for pedestrians.
(Photo: Devon County Council)

CONTEXT

The Plains is an important focal point of Totnes, lying to the west of the River Dart on one of the major approaches to this historic town. The eastern side of The Plains consists of a number of warehouses and other listed buildings which had fallen into disrepair, while the western side contains several listed buildings mainly in commercial use. The whole area was dominated by an excessive amount of carriageway space, largely devoted to parking and bus services. Pedestrians were afforded little space in this important part of the town.

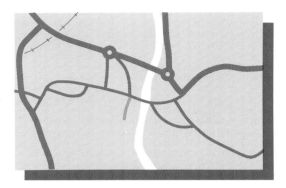

OBJECTIVES

In order to improve the quality of the environment in The Plains it was recognised that a substantial change of emphasis was required to reduce the domination of vehicles.

DESCRIPTION

Work was undertaken in two phases. Phase I involved the enhancement of Dartmouth Inn Square. This small square off the western side of The Plains was cluttered by some 22 car parking spaces. Measures included removing all the on-street parking and providing a pleasantly landscaped area where people can sit and relax or enjoy a drink from the recently refurbished Dartmouth Inn which gives the square its name.

Phase II constituted the major part of the enhancement works which involved the removal of the majority of the on-street parking, the relocation of the buses into extended bus lay-bys in nearby Coronation Road and the narrowing of the carriageway. The widened footways give considerably more space for safe pedestrian activity,

90

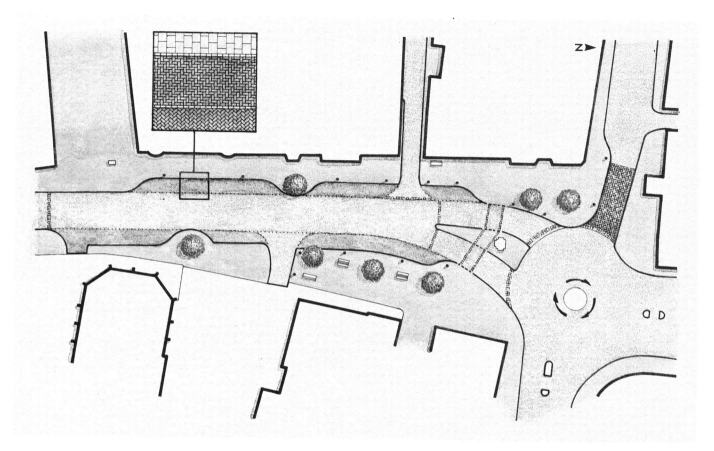

seating and signs, while the Wills Memorial island provides a much safer pedestrian route for people entering the town. The whole of The Plains area has also been the subject of a comprehensive lighting scheme increasing pedestrian safety and visibility.

COST

The cost of the refurbishment works was approximately £250,000.

ASSESSMENT

The scheme has achieved the objectives of helping to reduce vehicle speeds and providing larger safe areas for pedestrians. In addition, by removing much of the on-street parking and reducing the widths of the carriageway, pedestrian movements have been made considerably easier and safer. The environment has been greatly enhanced.

91: A planted central island marks the start of Dulmen Buldern village, and a banner creates an effective (though temporary) gateway effect. Separate cycle and footways are provided, even outside the village.
(Photo: T. Pharoah)

92: Planted areas alternately in the centre and at the side soften the street scene and create a lateral shift to help moderate vehicle speed.
(Photo: T. Pharoah)

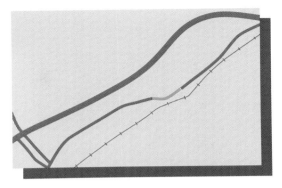

CONTEXT

During the 1980s the Nordrhein-Westfalen Ministry of Town Planning, Housing and Traffic undertook a study of safety and traffic calming possibilities on 27 village through roads (classified as Lander or Federal roads). The study was prompted by the fact that the average total cost of accidents on these roads was about 50% higher than that for all roads. Dulmen Buldern is an example, lying astride the B51 between Dortmund and Munster.

OBJECTIVES

The aim in Dulmen Buldern, as in the other experimental schemes, was primarily to reduce accidents and to reduce the dangers, intimidation, noise and fumes from motor traffic. All of these problems were of concern to the majority of residents interviewed. Particular concern was expressed about the dangers of crossing the road, especially for children going to school and nurseries.

DESCRIPTION

In Dulmen Buldern the following measures were implemented:
- Physical reduction of carriageway width
- Parking areas defined
- Central islands (planted) built at the village entries
- Central islands in the village centre with crossing points
- Road markings

91

92

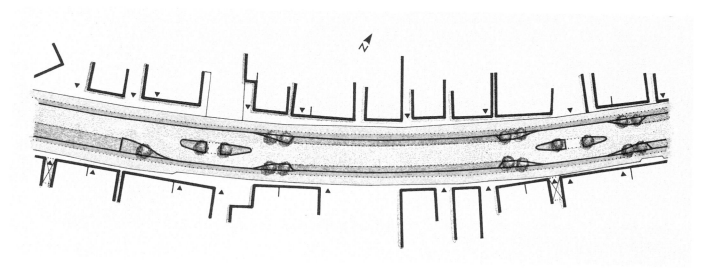

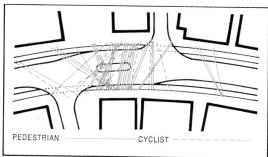

PEDESTRIAN ——————— CYCLIST - - - - -

CROSSING MOVEMENTS OF CYCLISTS AND PEDESTRIANS NEAR ISLAND

93

93: Broad central islands include tree planting, and provide comfortable shelter for pedestrians while enhancing the village atmosphere. (Photo: T. Pharoah)

- Planting of trees and shrubs
- Separate cycleways

COST

Not known.

ASSESSMENT

No separate data are available for Dulmen Buldern. "Before" studies of 15 similar through roads showed the average cost of accidents to be 50% higher than on all traffic roads, and 85 percentile speeds in village centres above the legal limit of 30 mph in every case. 85 percentile speeds at village entrances were even higher. Carriageway narrowing was found, by itself, not to have any appreciable effect on driving speeds. The results of other "after" studies are not yet available.

94: Entrance to Much village emphasized with a change of surface and stone walls.
(Photo: T. Pharoah)

95: Side roads are paved in brick, and the optical width of the through road is reduced by the use of tree planting either side. The stone wall feature is used in place of the standard traffic bollard.
(Photo: T. Pharoah)

MUCH · VILLAGE CENTRE · GERMANY

CONTEXT

The village of Much lies astride the B56 (Federal road) about 30 km east of Cologne. This through road carries about 6,000 vehicles per day of which up to 9% are lorries over 2.8 tonnes. There was no possibility of a bypass being built, and discussions with the public and relevant authorities ruled out the use of parallel residential roads to relieve the village centre.

OBJECTIVES

The original aim of the scheme's promoter (an officer in the Nordrhein-Westfalen roads authority) was to restrict traffic to improve conditions for cyclists.

The scheme eventually adopted had rather wider objectives of resolving the conflict between through traffic, the life of the village centre, and the general environment and character of the narrow main street. "Before" studies revealed that the situation was unsatisfactory in respect of the following:
- 85 percentile speeds over most of the through road were over 30 mph, with speeds over 40 mph at the village entrances
- 31 accidents in three and a half years including 1 death and 21 injuries.

94

95

- Street noise 70-75 dBA
- No separate path for cyclists
- Footways less than 1m width in the village centre

Opinion surveys showed 60% of residents dissatisfied with the situation, 80% wanting traffic calming measures, and only 10% considering action to be unnecessary.

DESCRIPTION

The overall appearance and character of the village did not allow partial reconstruction or simple measures, mainly because of tight spatial dimensions. The scheme implemented during 1987-89 consisted of a reordering of street space to include progressive reduction of the carriageway width towards the village centre, and further "optical" reduction using tree planting and side strips. At key positions, walls in natural stone were built as architectural features either side of the carriageway. Junctions were also remodeled to give greater priority to pedestrians and cyclists, and road humps were installed on adjacent village streets to avoid traffic diversions. A unique feature was the reduction in the width of the carriageway in the busiest part of the village to 4.5m, a width not normally allowed on Federal roads. This means that two cars can pass but not two large vehicles. For the latter, right of way applies to vehicles leaving the centre. There were also fairly long stretches of 5.5m - 6m, rather than the usual 6.5m. Separate cycleways were provided adjacent to the footway on the wider stretches.

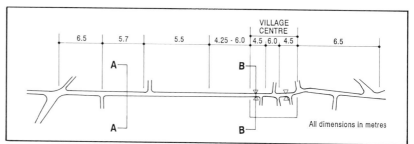

CARRIAGEWAY WIDTHS, MUCH VILLAGE THROUGH ROAD

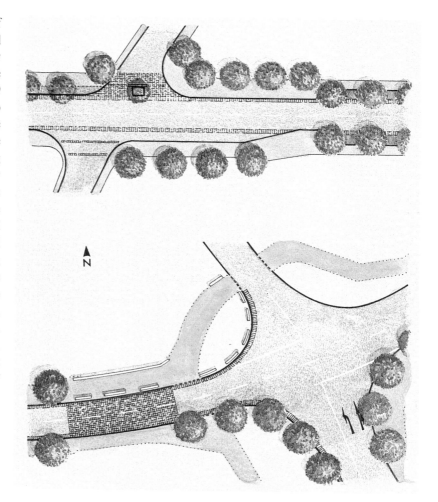

96: The carriageway constrictions of 4.5m (unusual for a Federal road) are defined by walls in natural stone in the centre of the village. Note also the parking bays paved in lighter colour. (Photo: T. Pharoah)

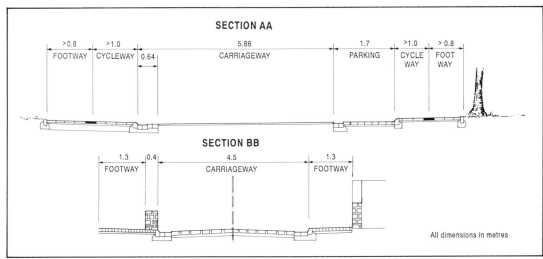

CROSS SECTIONS THROUGH FOOTWAY AND CARRIAGEWAY

96

COST

The cost of the entire scheme involving about 1.7 km of street length was about £1.7 million including 20% for architectural features such as walls in natural stone. In the main the works were funded by Nordrhein-Westfalen. Research costs were met by the Federal Roads Agency (BaST).

ASSESSMENT

Not yet available.

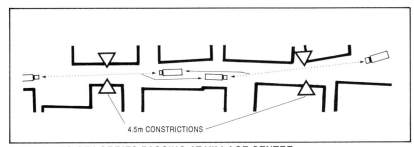

SIGHT LINES OF LORRIES PASSING AT VILLAGE CENTRE

REFERENCE DOCUMENTS

Civic Trust, County Surveyors Society, Department of Transport, **Lorries and Traffic Management/Lorries in the community** (1990).

Department of the Environment, Department of Transport, **Residential Roads and Footpaths.** Design Bulletin 32 (1977, revised edition being prepared).

Department of Transport, **Cyclists at Road Crossings and Junctions.** Local Transport Note 1/86.

Department of Transport, **Shared use by Cyclists and Pedestrians.** Local Transport Note 2/86.

Department of Transport, **Making way for Cyclists.** Local Transport Note 1/89.

Department of Transport, **Children and Roads: A Safer Way** (1990).

Department of Transport, **Road Humps.** Circular Roads 3/90.

Department of Transport, **20 mph Speed Limit Zones.** Circular Roads 4/90.

Department of Transport, **Speed Control Humps.** Traffic Advisory Leaflet 2/90.

Department of Transport, **Urban Safety Management Guidelines from IHT.** Traffic Advisory Leaflet 3/90.

Devon County Council, **Residential Estates Design Guide** (1989).

Institution of Highways and Transportation, **Providing for People with a Mobility Handicap, Guidelines** (1986, revised edition being prepared).

Institution of Highways and Transportation, Department of Transport, **Roads and Traffic in Urban Areas** (1987).

Institution of Highways and Transportation, **Urban Safety Management, Guidelines** (1990).

Institution of Highways and Transportation, **Accident Reduction and Prevention, Guidelines** (1990).

Institution of Highways and Transportation, **The Safety Audit of Highways, Guidelines** (1990).

Local Authority Associations, **Road Safety Code of Good Practice** (1989).

Organisation for Economic Cooperation and Development, **Integrated Traffic Safety Management in Urban Areas** (1990).

Statutory Instruments 1990 No. 703, **The Highways (Road Humps) Regulations 1990.**